Ignite Your Email Campaign

A ministryTHRIVE Production

© 2018 by John D. Leavy

All rights reserved.

Reproduction or translation of any part of this work beyond that permitted by Section 107 or 108 of the 1976 United States Copyright Act without permission of the copyright owner is unlawful. Requests for permission or further information should be emailed to: John D. Leavy at john@ministryTHRIVE.com.

This publication is designed to provide accurate and authoritative information regarding the subject matter covered. It is sold with the understanding that the publisher or author are not engaged in rendering legal, accounting or other professional services. If legal advice or other expert assistance is required, the services of a competent professional person should be sought.

ISBN-13:
978-1725618862 (John D. Leavy)

ISBN-10:
1725618869

First Printing: August 2018

Printed in the United States of America

*"Therefore, my beloved brethren,
be steadfast, immovable, always abounding
in the work of the Lord, knowing that your toil
is not in vain in the Lord."*

1 Corinthians 15:58

Ignite Your Email Campaign

Contents

Introduction 8

PART I
Before You Go Live

1: What Goes into an Email Campaign? 13

2: Why Email Campaigns in the First Place? 19

3: Don't Email Campaigns Need Email Addresses? 27

PART II
Mapping Out Your Email Campaign Strategy

4: Achieving Your Goals 35

5: Preparing the Action Plan 45

6: Readying the Team 51

7: Executing the Plan 56

8: Monitoring and Learning 61

9: Testing and Adapting 65

PART III

Writing Action-driven Content

10: Writing with a Purpose 72

11: Personalizing Your Message 99

12: *"Pay No Attention to the Man Behind the Curtain"* 102

13: Staying Donor-focused 106

14: Empowering with Trigger Words 109

15: Delivering Value 111

16: Skipping the Non-profit Lingo 115

17: Calling Readers to Act 117

PART IV

Delivering and Tracking Your Campaigns

18: Choosing an Email Platform 122

19: Uploading Your Contacts 126

20: Creating Your First Campaign 130

21: Making Sense of the Reports 147

22: Fine-tuning the Campaign 150

23: Sending Video Messages 160

PART V

"The Payoff"

24: Announcing an Event by Email 164
25: Doing a Giveaway by Email 172
26: Making an Appeal by Email 183
27: Delivering a Newsletter by Email 196
28: Sharing a Blog Post by Email 213

29: Before I Go 221

Introduction

Ignite Your Email Campaign is the only resource you'll ever need when building and executing email campaigns that produce phenomenal results. Phenomenal results that are reproducible again and again.

The sole purpose of *Ignite Your Email Campaign* is to aid in your success. The goals in writing this book were simple, help ministries and non-profits leverage email campaigns to boost cause awareness, increase name acquisition, build lasting relationships, and raise more money. If these are the objectives of your organization—then look no further. Start reading *Ignite Your Email Campaign* now.

Ignite Your Email Campaign targets several audiences: those organizations that are currently running email campaigns but are looking to exploit this technology more. Second, *Ignite Your Email Campaign* is directed at those groups that need to fine-tune their campaigns to gain more sustainable results. And last, to those individuals that are beginning to investigate email campaigns as a means of engaging their donors and potential supporters.

Boosting cause awareness, increasing name acquisition, building relationships, and raising money are all connected. Before one can increase name acquisition, the organization must engage in making people aware of their cause. Before they can fundraise, they must build strong relationships with potential supporters.

An organization can never stop trumpeting the cause, acquiring new contacts to educate and engage, develop strong relationships, and in the end, hopefully these activities generate revenue, so the organization can continue to impact lives.

The four activities are connected in a cyclical pattern of effort that needs to take place on an ongoing basis.

Once the motivation, the goals, are identified, the momentum shifts to the Message, crafting the actionable content. Once the messaging is complete the focus shifts to Method. How will the message be sent to the audiences?

Ignite Your Campaign is divided into five parts. Begin where the feeling strikes you. If you're just starting out, then Part I is a perfect beginning point. Part II is devoted to developing a solid email campaign strategy. Part III talks about writing action-driven content. Part IV discusses launching and tracking your campaigns. And Part V finishes with The Payoff, the reasons why you purchased *Ignite Your Email Campaign*. You want to Boost Cause Awareness, Increase Name Acquisition, Build Stronger Relationships, and Raise More Money.

What an Email Campaign Is Not

What an Email Campaign Is Not separates the planners from the procrastinators. The occasional email sent out when one *has the time* hardly fits our model of an email campaign. A single email sent out at the end of the year does not fit our model as well. Then there are the emails sent out almost regularly, perhaps eight or nine months out of year. That's not what *Ignite Your Email Campaign* endorses. We're going to be talking about email campaigns that are: premeditated, strategic, well-designed promotions.

How could a new friendship take hold if two individuals spoke once and then never again? How could a friendship grow if the two people hardly conversed?

Effective email campaigns are well-thought out, planned, scheduled, orchestrated, set of events where an organization communicates and engages its audience with purpose.

Successful, effective email campaigns don't just happen. They take sweat equity. Enough said.

You'll find loads of Tips and Show & Tell Examples and worksheets throughout *Ignite Your Email Campaign*.

Tips such as, "Personalize your email salutation" helps people take advantage of what's most successful.

Show & Tell: There are dozens of Examples and Worksheets—the Worksheets are editable, so you'll be able to instantly apply what you've learned.

Change Tomorrow!

John D. Leavy
President
ministryTHRIVE.com

john@ministrythrive.com

PART I

Before You Go Live

Chapter 1...

What Goes into an Email Campaign?
(7 MIN READ)

*W*hat *Goes into an Email Campaign* breaks the process down into its discrete components: **goals, metrics,** the **message, names, an offer, the email delivery system, landing pages, timing, results, and frequency**. Not to worry, if some of these terms seem unfamiliar. They'll become good friends as you discover how to build and execute your own email campaigns.

Of course, almost anything an organization sets out to do requires goals. Setting goals is talked about in Chapter 4. For now, let's dissect the balance of the elements found in a typical email campaign.

The Ingredients of an Email Campaign

1. **Metrics –** Metrics: a method of measuring something. Metrics are the numbers that separate gut feelings from reality. It's of little value to *think* or *feel* the

   > *"Metrics are the numbers that separate gut feelings from reality."*

   email campaign is accomplishing the goals. Numbers tell whether the objectives are being reached. We talk in more detail about metrics later in *Ignite Your Email Campaign*, but for now let's understand that some numbers will be more actionable, others not so much. For example, people that open an email require no immediate action. On the other hand, people that download our free eBook have shown a high level of interest and need following up.

2. **Action-driven Content (The Message) –** The emails sent out need to showcase the purpose of the communique. The messages need to be relevant, timely, and purposeful. The email content should be brief and enticing without being boring. The content should be compelling and action-driven.

    Tip: Make every effort to have the email sound like you're writing to each person individually.

3. **Names (Recipients, Subscribers)** – Don't send everyone in your contact file the same message. Know your audience. Donors will obviously want a deeper information dive than those unfamiliar with the organization. If the contact file contains major donors, regular supporters, and potential donors, then three versions of the email messages need to be developed. Each recipient group has a different commitment level.

4. **The Offer** – Offers entice people to act. Offer an early-bird discount or a free gift to encourage people to subscribe, join, or donate. Make sure what's being given away is of *real* value to the person receiving the free gift. If the giveaway is not performing well, then swap it out for something else. This is a perfect opportunity to see which gift performs best.

5. **Email Delivery System** – Launching email campaigns and relying on "gut feelings" as to how well things went does not work. Instead rely on the comprehensive reports generated by an email automation platform such as MailChimp or ConstantContact. How will the organization know who and how many recipients open the email? How will they be able to tell how many messages were read and who clicked through to the offer? Yes, it will be obvious how many subscribers were generated, but will the organization know how many people clicked-through to the offer and then bailed, no? MailChimp, for instance, offers their service free

forever as long as the organization does not email more than 2,000 recipients.

6. **The Timing** – Timing will be a guessing game each organization must play. Conventional wisdom might say Tuesday mornings between 9:00 and 10:30 Central Standard Time is the optimal window to email folks. True as this may be for some organizations, others may opt to send out emails at different times thinking if no one else is trying to attract people's interest, perhaps we may have a shot. It boils down to—know your audience members.

Tip: Run campaign tests to see if mornings generate a better open-rate than afternoons and if Tuesdays generate more interest than Thursday or Fridays.

7. **The Results** – Awhile back, I wrote an article titled, *Vanity Numbers verses Actionable Metrics*. Some numbers are important, other numbers are more important. It' good to know how many recipients opened the email that was sent. It's more crucial to know how many of those people clicked-through to the landing page that held the free offer. Finally, the number of people that actually acted and subscribed, joined, or donated, is the most useful. Choose the

> *"Some numbers are important, other number are more important."*

numbers to watch closely. In the end, are the numbers being monitored helping the organization achieve its goals?

8. **The Frequency** – Let's separate Timing from Frequency. Timing refers to when the email is sent. Frequency deals with how many and how often emails are dispatched. There are organizations that communicate at no particular frequency. This practice probably produces the poorest results. Other organizations communicate once a quarter while still others may communicate several times per week. Here's a question to ponder, "Which organization do you believe is upper-most in the recipient's mind?" Yep, the one that emails the most. Is this the best practice, maybe? Again, each organization needs to decide on its own frequency for emailing its contacts.

9. **Landing Page** – A landing page is a standalone web page. It's where the email recipient lands when clicking the link embedded within the message. At the landing page, the recipient can learn more about the event being announced or the free gift being given away. Do not make the mistake of sending people to the organization's homepage expecting people to hunt for the free offer create a landing page, instead. Unbounce.com, a premier company in this landing page space, offers a 30-day free trial of its software, free customer support, a drag and drop page builder, built-in conversion tools, and more.

Anatomy of an Email Campaign

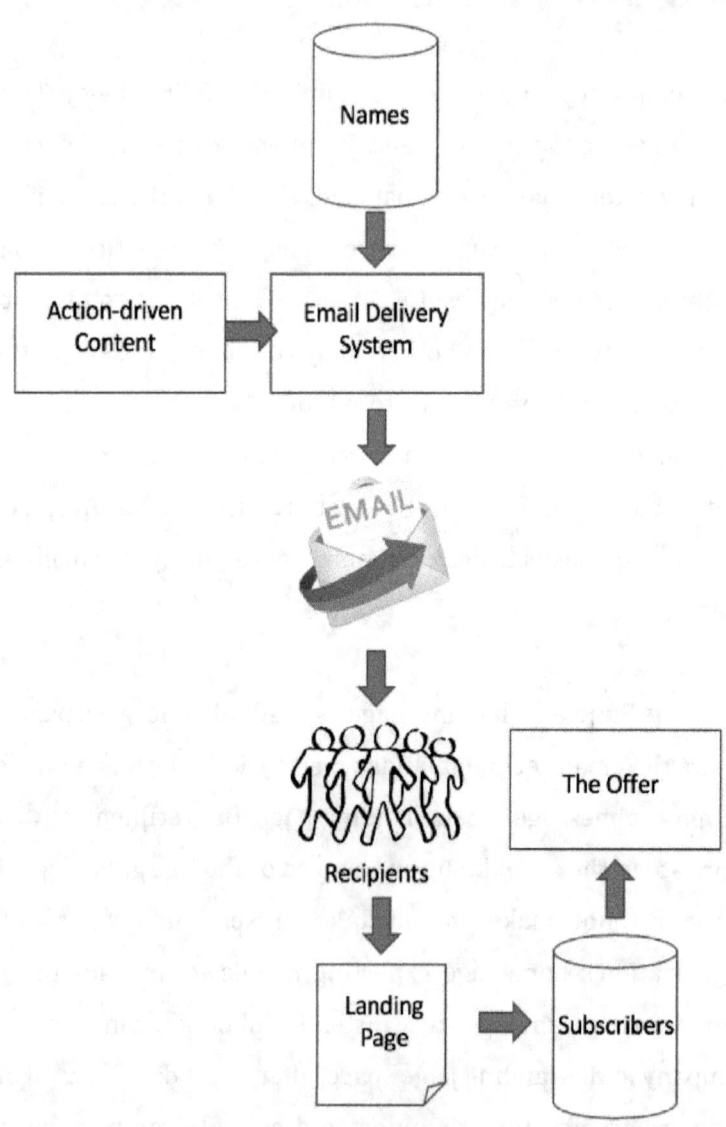

Chapter 2...

Why Email Campaigns in the First Place?

(7 MIN READ)

E mailing is an inexpensive way to reach individuals as well as large and small audiences. The ramp-up time for an email campaign is short and takes little technical know-how. With time, patience, and testing you'll be able to tell if email campaigns are a good way to communicate your message.

Tip: Email campaigns can be personalized which helps bolster the relationship between the sender and receiver.

Did you know?
205 billion emails are sent each day. **246 billion** is the expected number by 2019.

Email Still Tops the List of Engagement Tools

Certainly, face-to-face meetings will always be rated the most effective way to communicate with an individual or group. But let's turn our attention to communicating with hundreds or thousands of people located miles apart.

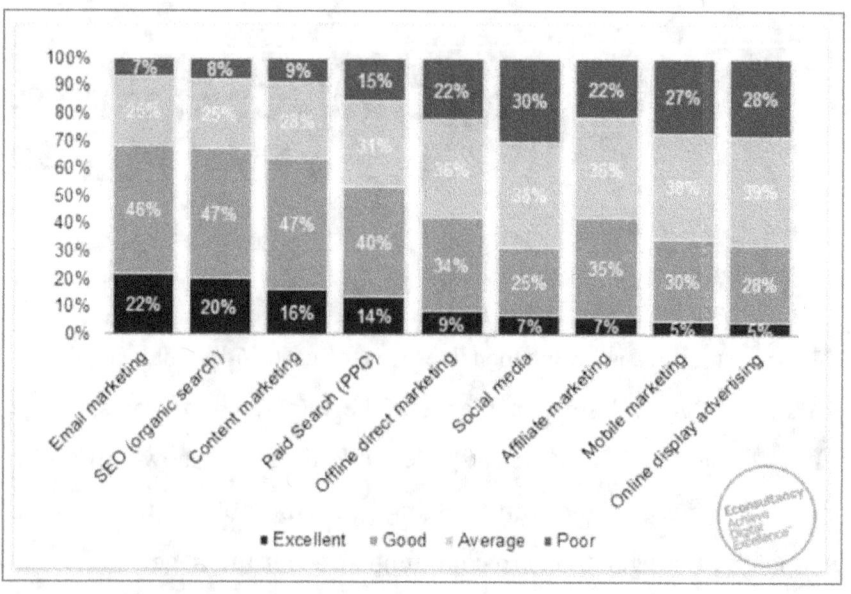

The following statistics are quite compelling on the side for choosing email campaigns as a preferred method for reaching out to people. These numbers were compiled courtesy of EmailMonks.com:

- **Personalization in the email body** has an open-rate of 29.95% and a click-through rate of 5.03%. (GetResponse)

- **Personalize Subject lines** lift the open-rates by 29.3% (MarketingSherpa)
- 47% of email recipients open email **based on the Subject line** (Invesp)
- **72% of customers open an email** due to the discount it offers and 62% of customers open due to the personalized Subject line (Campaign Monitor)
- In 2017, **the average results for email campaigns across industries** were: Open-rate 24.79%, Click-through Rate 4.19%, and Click-to-open rate 11.88% (SmartInsights)
- **Emails that include some sort of graphics** (pictures or images) have a higher open-rate (26.89%) and higher click-through rate (4.36%) than that of text-based emails (getResponse)

Of course, everyone's campaign statistical percentages will vary depending upon the email content, format, timing, offer, target audience, and other variables.

If some of the terms used above are unfamiliar, here's a quick primer on the metrics tracked by most email automation programs:

Bounce – the percentage of visitors to a particular website who navigate away from the site after viewing only one page.

Chick-through – the action or facility of following a hypertext link to a particular website.

Open-rate – percentage for an email sent to multiple recipients is then most often calculated as the total number of "opened" emails, expressed as a percentage of the total number of emails sent or—more usually—delivered.

Unsubscribe – cancels a subscription to an electronic mailing list or online service.

 Tip: The responsibility lies with each organization to test, test, and test until the best possible campaign results are achieved.

Email Campaign Dos and Don'ts

The email practice we're endorsing does not infer spamming people. If you're unfamiliar with the CAN-SPAM Act of 2003 here are the Dos and Don'ts.

Do not assume the following information is in any way legal advice or counsel. Consult the Federal Trade Commission (FTC) website for the details.

DO:

- Include a valid mailing address in all emails being sent out

- Create an obvious way for a recipient to opt-out of any further communiques
- The "From," "To," and "Reply" must clearly state who is sending the message

DON'T:

- Do not sell or transfer any recipient's email address
- Do not make it difficult for a recipient to unsubscribe
- Do not use deceptive Subject lines that misrepresent the contents of the message

In the following chart from MarketingSherpa.com on how customers prefer to communicate, email is in the lead by a large margin:

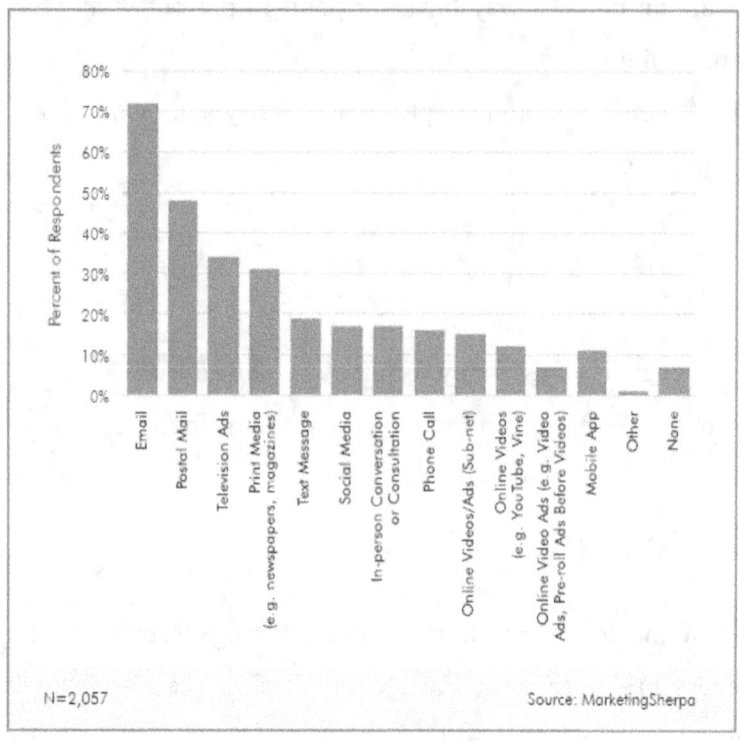

Each organization needs to determine if email is an approach they want to employ when reaching out to its donors and potential supporters.

The Email Campaign Skills

So what skills are needed to execute a successful email campaign?

In an article on Entrepreneur.com, Vikas Lalwani, in *8 Ingredients of an Off-the-Charts Email Marketing Campaign*, highlights these elements:

- A clear objective
- An interesting Subject line
- A well thought out message
- An appealing design
- A compelling call-to-action
- A dedicated landing page
- The right time to send
- Testing, testing, testing

Let's add some modest writing ability, sprinkled with a little knowledge of marketing and technology to this list. From here, you should be well on your way to creating action-driven email campaigns that produce positive results.

People May Not Be Listening

If an organization has not been communicating with its audience members on a regular basis expect the open and click-through rates to be low at first, perhaps even non-existent. People may not be used to hearing from you.

Here's an illustration. Each time you take a walk around your neighborhood you pass by people without saying hello. Then you

> *"People may not be used to hearing from you."*

decide to start acknowledging their existence as you pass. You start saying, "Good Afternoon" and they respond back—most of them anyway. The lesson here is, the more you engage people the more they respond back, it's human nature.

Emailing folks is not much different. You email your contacts on a regular basis, and they'll start answering back.

 Tip: The more you communicate with people on a regular basis the more responsive they become.

Consistency is one of the secret ingredients to getting people to reply to the emails you send.

Chapter 3...

Don't Email Campaigns Need Email Addresses?
(7 MIN READ)

Ever read articles with titles such as, "Growing Your Email List by 1,000 New Subscribers Is a No-brainer," or "How to Acquire Hundreds of New Donors Without Really Trying," or "75 Proven Ways to Add More Email Addresses to Your Contact File."

> *"There is no easy way to acquire new email addresses."*

 Tip: There is no easy way to acquire new email addresses.

It takes work, lots of work, hard work. If it was as easy as some people write about there wouldn't be 703,000 results that come up when a person Googles "grow your email list."

Suppose we look at ways individuals and organizations can acquire new email addresses. There are practical methods online as well as offline. Let's examine both.

You Have to Start Somewhere

Let's say we set a goal of acquiring 1,000 new names and email addresses within the next 60 days. Of course, we'll want these names to be of potential supporters, volunteers, donors, or someone who has the same passion we do.

Here we go...

- We could go through the contacts on our smart phone to see if anyone is a potential candidate. Don't eliminate anyone. Let each person eliminate them self.
- If we like to write, we could search out guest blogging opportunities or write for our local paper.
- We could contact family, friends, cousins, as well as other relatives.
- Don't forget the people you work with now or have worked with in the past.
- We could export our LinkedIn connection's email addresses and send them ONE email to see if they show any interest in what the organization is doing.

- How about the professionals that touch our lives every day: our doctors, accountant, and other professionals?
- Make sure to always collect and share business cards at offline events.
- Write an email announcing what you're up to and ask your current email contacts to forward the message.
- Create a giveaway and post it on your website. Have people register for a contest.
- Host a free webinar.
- Create subscriber-only discounts for your website and blog.
- Ask your social media followers.
- Seek interviews on your local TV and radio stations.
- Your acquaintances at church (past churches?)
- Those from small groups you've attended.
- Neighbors (past neighbors?)
- Those you work with (past business associates?)
- Friends from college.
- Friends from social, civic, or professional organizations.
- Contractors (plumbers, heating & air conditioning specialists, landscapers, handymen).
- You could use your Facebook page or run ads on Facebook to acquire new email addresses.
- You could run a survey or contest on Twitter to acquire the new names.
- You could promote offers on Pinterest.

- You could leverage your organization's YouTube channel.
- You could form strategic partnerships with likeminded organizations to cross-promote each other.
- Don't forget to send emails to the addresses you do have. Give them a free gift and ask them to forward your email to their friends.

Tip: Don't SPAM people. Don't just add people's email addresses to your distribution list without their permission.

This work may seem daunting but collecting email addresses is not easy.

"Don't just add people's email addresses to your distribution list without their permission."

Don't ask people for more personal information than you initially plan to use. It's only natural for the individual to think they'll receive something in the mail if they give up their street address.

List building is an activity that can never stop.

If you only have a few dozen addresses in your contact file, you have some serious work ahead of you, so roll up your sleeves.

 **Show & Tell:** Find both a Fundraising Software Email Campaign and an Event Dinner Email Campaign Example at the end of this chapter.

Fundraising Software Email Campaign Example

**Fundraising Software
Email Campaign Example**

A company offers a free trial of their fundraising software. They decide to send out eight e-mails during a free trial process. Any interested individual can opt-out of the email campaign at any time. It does not affect their ability to complete the free trial.

The company plans to advertise a free-trial of the software on their website, newsletter, and through social media.

Here's how the eight-email campaign is structured:

Email 1 sent out when someone signs up for the free trial. Confirms sign-up.

Email 2 sent out on Day 1. Welcomes the new subscriber to the free trial process.

Email 3 sent out on Day 3. Focus on a major feature that benefits the individual or organization.

Email 4 sent out on Day 7. Focus on a major feature that benefits the individual or organization.

Email 5 sent out on Day 11. Focus on a major feature that benefits the individual or organization.

Email 6 sent out on Day 13. Focus on a major feature that benefits the individual or organization.

Email 7 sent out on Day 15. Informs the prospect that the free trial is expiring.

Email 8 sent out on Day 17. Tells the individual a special offer is available if the purchase is made.

This email campaign strategy is nonthreatening because the prospect can opt-out at any time. The emails keep the person engaged with compelling information about important benefit-driven features of the software product. At the end of the trial the person can either purchase the software product or not.

Copyright © 2018 ministryTHRIVE

Download at:

ministryTHRIVE.com/IYE/FundraisingSoftwareExample.pdf

Event Dinner
Email Campaign Example

**Event Dinner
Email Campaign Example**

An organization plans on having their annual fundraising dinner in November. They decide to send out six e-mails during their campaign. Any disinterested party can opt-out of the email campaign at any time.

Here's how the six-email campaign is structured:

Email 1 sent out 6 weeks before the dinner – Announces the annual dinner and offers early-bird discount dinner tickets.

Email 2 sent out 5 weeks before the dinner – Introduces the keynote speaker and mentions the early-bird discount is ending.

Email 3 sent out 4 weeks before the dinner – Highlights the impact and progress the organization has made over the past year.

Email 4 sent out 3 weeks before the dinner – Encourages donors to continue their valued support and invites potential supports to join the cause.

Email 5 sent out 2 weeks before the dinner – Includes testimonials from past attenders and what the work of the organization has meant to them personally.

Email 6 sent out 1 week before the dinner – Plea from key board member or major donor on how lives are being changed and why the work must continue.

This email campaign strategy is nonthreatening because the email recipients can opt-out at any time. The emails keep the person engaged with compelling information, stories, and testimonials. In the end, the person can either attend the dinner or skip the event.

Copyright © 2018 ministryTHRIVE

Download at:

ministryTHRIVE.com/IYE/EventDinnerExample.pdf

PART II

Mapping Out Your Email Campaign Strategy

Chapter 4...

Achieving Your Goals

(6 MIN READ)

Goals need to be specific, measurable, attainable, realistic, and time bound. These qualifiers come from the SMART goal setting method. "Raise more funds" or "acquire more names" are hardly specific goals. Whereas, "acquire 1,000 new names in the next 60 days is specific, measurable, and time bound. But, is the goal *realistic* and *attainable*? Only time and effort will tell.

Setting Specific Goals

You may want to set three specific goals for your email campaign: 1.) goals for existing donors and potential supporters,

2.) goals for acquiring the email addresses of new potential patrons, 3.) and goals for the email campaign itself.

For instance, you might set the goal of raising a certain five or six figure sum of money during the campaign. A second goal might be to acquire 1,000 new email addresses, so you can inform, educate, and nurture those contacts over a certain time period. And last, you may want to strive for a 30% open-rate and a 6% click-through rate on the emails sent out.

These goals are all specific, measurable, and time bound. The realistic and attainable parts are yet to be determined. Here are other specific, measurable goal examples:

- Increase the size of your donor list by 20%.
- Increase the number of donors that do direct deposit by 20%.
- Increase the number of monthly donors by 10%.
- Acquire one more major donor.

Setting Measurable Goals

It will be easy to tell if the financial goal is being met by checking the bank account. It will also be obvious how many new email addresses are being acquired. MailChimp.com can automatically add the new addresses to a contact file if one was created during the campaign process. (More on this later.)

We'll be able to measure the success of the email campaign itself using the reports generated by the email automation platform we chose.

The basic MailChimp.com report tells us: How many emails were sent out, how many were received successfully, and how many bounced because the email address was invalid. The report highlights: how many emails were opened and how many individuals clicked on the links within the email message. The report goes on to tell us how many people unsubscribed, forwarded our message, and how well our email performed against the national average for our industry setting such as "non-profit."

Here's a sample MailChimp.com report snippet:

Open rate	43.6%	Click rate	12%
List avg	35.1%	List avg	7.4%
Industry avg	19.4%	Industry avg	1.6%
4,969	1,368	17	2
Opened	Clicked	Bounced	Unsubscribed

Setting Attainable Goals

Setting attainable goals will always be a work-in-progress. If past email campaign numbers are not available all one can do is, make their best guesstimate. As time passes during the execution of the campaign, it will become obvious if the numbers chosen can be reached. For example, if acquiring 3,000 new email addresses over a 90-day period was the goal, and only 550 new addresses were acquired 30 days in, it should be apparent the goal of 3,000 new contacts may be out of reach.

If the organization has historical data from past campaigns, it will be easier to judge what numbers are likely attainable on future campaigns.

Time will tell.

> *"Things change from year to year. The progress made in the past is no guarantee for future results."*

Things change from year to year. The progress made in the past is no guarantee for future results.

Setting Realistic Goals

Attainable goals are more of a yardstick-measurement during the execution of a campaign. The old: "Are we there yet?"

Realistic is more a function of what's reasonable to expect for a campaign. An organization that raises under $10,000 one year cannot increase their goal to raise $100,000 the next year without making dramatic changes to their email campaign process.

Perhaps answering these two questions will assist in setting realistic goals: "What have we done historically?" and "What have other organizations our size achieved?"

 Tip: There's nothing wrong with setting the bar high. Just make sure the organization can clear the bar.

Setting Time Bound Goals

People need deadlines. How else will the team know they've arrived at the end? They've completed what was set before them? Donors need deadlines. They need to know the campaign to raise funds will come to an end some day and the work to change lives will start.

Don't set deadline so far into the future that the team and donors lose track of time. Set intermediate milestones to show that progress is being made. If the fundraising campaign lasts all year, then publish monthly and quarterly progress reports. These reports can be used to create urgency if progress toward the goal is lagging.

 **Show & Tell:** Find both a Project Priority Example and Worksheet, and a SMART Goal Setting Example and Worksheet at the end of this chapter.

Project Priority Example

Project Priority Example

Ignite Your End-of-the-year Fundraising webinar
for ABC Global Foundation on July 24, 2018

Project One: Create slides for Ignite Your End-of-the-year Fundraising webinar for ABC Global Foundation.

Urgency: July 6, 2018   Cost: _____   Priority: 1

Project Two: Create landing pages to register for free digital copy of Ignite Your End-of-the-year Fundraising.

Urgency: July 9, 2018   Cost: _____   Priority: 2

Project Three: Do webinar run through with ABC Global Foundation host.

Urgency: July 10, 2018   Cost: _____   Priority: 3

Project Four: Do Ignite Your End-of-the-year Fundraising webinar on July 24, 2018.

Urgency: July 24, 2018   Cost: _____   Priority: 4

Project Five: Create landing pages to register LinkedIn connections to view webinar on Vimeo and receive free digital copy of Ignite Your End-of-the-year Fundraising.

Urgency: July 31, 2018   Cost: _____   Priority: 5

Copyright © 2018 ministryTHRIVE

Download at:
ministryTHRIVE.com/IYE/ProjectPriorityExample.pdf

Ignite Your Email Campaign

Project Priority Worksheet

```
Project Priority Worksheet

Brief Project Description

Project One: _____
_____

Urgency: _____    Cost: _____    Priority: _____

Project Two: _____
_____

Urgency: _____    Cost: _____    Priority: _____

Project Three: _____
_____

Urgency: _____    Cost: _____    Priority: _____

Project Four: _____
_____

Urgency: _____    Cost: _____    Priority: _____

Project Five: _____
_____

Urgency: _____    Cost: _____    Priority: _____


Copyright © 2018 ministryTHRIVE
```

Download at:
ministryTHRIVE.com/IYE/ProjectPriorityWorksheet.docx

Ignite Your Email Campaign

SMART Goal Setting Example

SMART Goal Setting Example
ABC Global Foundation

Project One:
Prepare and present a webinar on Ignite Your End-of-the-year Fundraising. To attract attendees, a free digital copy of Ignite Your End-of-the-year Fundraising will be given away to all those that register and/or attend the webinar on July 24, 2018. Following the webinar presentation, an email blast will be sent out to 2,000 LinkedIn connections to acquire new subscription to THRIVE5 (the weekly news brief). Statistics will be gather for the webinar and the LinkedIn email blast.

Specific:
The slides will be prepared in PowerPoint. The webinar presentation will be done in ZOOM. ABC Global Foundation will track webinar attendees. ministryTHRIVE will track email downloads. The presentation is expected to run 45 minutes. 40 to 45 slides will be needed to explain the eight chapters in Ignite Your End-of-the-year Fundraising. It is important the webinar be available on-demand. Later on, the on-demand webinar will be used as a marketing tool to acquire more new email addresses and other webinar presentation opportunities.

Measurable:
ABC Global Foundation will track webinar invites, registration, and attendance through ZOOM. MailChimp will be used to track emails to LinkedIn connections.

Attainable:
Potential webinar invites: 140
The webinar registrations: 70
The webinar attendees: 35
Email addresses and free digital downloads: 17
LinkedIn emails to send: 2,000
LinkedIn free digital downloads: 70 (3.5%)
THRIVE5 subscriptions: 70

Relevant:
Book chapters: Deciding on Your Fundraising Goals, Acquiring New Donors, Telling a Great Story, Getting Your Message Out, Setting Things in Motion, Following Up, Measuring Your Progress, and Getting Better Results. Mid-July is the perfect window to start talking about EOY fundraising.

Time Bound:
Complete slides by July 6. Complete landing pages by July 9. Do webinar run-through on July 10. Do webinar on July 24. Create LinkedIn landing pages and send emails by July 31, 2018.

Results:
The webinar invites: 140
The webinar registrations: 68
The webinar attendees: 31
Email addresses and free digital downloads: 21 (68% conversion rate)
THRIVE5 subscriptions: 21
LinkedIn emails sent: 2,000
LinkedIn free digital downloads: 140 (7%)
THRIVE5 subscriptions: 140

Copyright © 2018 ministryTHRIVE

Download at:
ministryTHRIVE.com/IYE/SMARTGoalSettingExample.pdf

Ignite Your Email Campaign

SMART Goal Setting Worksheet

SMART Goal Setting Worksheet

Brief Project Description

Project One: _____

Specific: _____

Measurable: _____

Attainable: _____

Relevant: _____

Time Bound: _____

Copyright © 2018 ministryTHRIVE

Download at:
ministryTHRIVE.com/IYE/SMARTGoalSettingWorksheet.docx

Chapter 5...

Preparing the Action Plan
(5 MIN READ)

Now that the goals are set, a plan (strategy) to achieve those objectives needs to be developed. Plans can be simple or complex. They can have a half-dozen steps or be more complicated. You make the choice. Go with whatever variation suits your organization best.

Organizations that are more mature and better staffed may opt to achieve their goals by using their website, social media channels, along with email campaigns.

Suppose we focus on using just email campaigns to achieve our stated goals.

Plans are typically comprised of these ingredients: goals, objectives, skills, responsibilities, schedules (timing and deadlines), resources, and budget.

Let's take a moment to define some terms so we're all on the same page. The **goal** is the outcome we hope to achieve. The **strategy** is the plan, or approach, employed to achieve the goal. An **objective** is a measurable step one takes to accomplish the overall strategy.

Suppose we set a goal of adding 1,000 new email addresses to our contact file over the next 60 days.

With that in mind, we might run a series of four email campaigns over the 60-day timeframe. Each campaign could be considered an *objective*.

Now, that we've settled on the goals and objectives questions, it's on to: skills, responsibilities, schedules, resources, and budget.

> *"It's vital the organization makes every effort to match the responsibilities to the people that have the necessary skills."*

It's vital the organization make every effort to match the **responsibilities** to people that have the necessary **skills**. Don't ask the person with little or no technical know-how to handle the responsibilities of running the email automation platform.

In the same vain, if there is a person who dislikes writing, they will not make the best candidate to draft the email messages.

As to **schedules** and meeting **deadlines,** it is essential these objectives are reached, and reached on time. Sending out a series of emails with no timetable in mind only confuses the recipients and will not produce the desired results.

Timing is just as important. Let's say the best time to send the emails out is between nine and ten o-clock in the morning on Tuesdays, Wednesdays or Thursday. So, sending the messages out late Friday afternoon will surely spell disaster for the campaign.

Here's a sample plan. We'll talk more about this in Chapter 7: *Executing the Plan.* It mentions the email number, the timing, and the purpose of the communique (for a free training session).

- Email 1. Sent out upon registering for the free training. This email confirms their sign-up.
- Email 2. Sent out on Day 1. Welcomes the student.
- Email 3. Sent out on Day 3. Focuses on a major feature that benefits the student.
- Email 4. Sent out on Day 7. Focuses on a second major feature.
- Email 5. Sent out on Day 11. Focuses on a third major feature.
- Email 6. Sent out on Day 13. Focuses on a fourth major feature.

- Email 7. Sent out on Day 15. Let's the student know the free trial is expiring.
- Email 8. Sent out on Day 17. Makes the student aware of a special offer if he or she enrolls.

Finally, there's the issue of **budget**. Luckily, many of the email automation platforms have free trials or free-forever memberships. For instance, at the writing of this book, MailChimp.com offers the best free-forever option as long as the organization does not email more than 2,000 contacts. iContact.com has a 30-day free trial while ConstantContact.com offers a free 60-day experience.

 **Show & Tell:** Find an Action Plan Example at the end of this chapter.

Ignite Your Email Campaign

Action Plan Schedule Example

	A	B	C	D	E	F
1			Action Plan Schedule Example			
2	July '18	Task	Person	Deadline	Actual	Comments
3	Week 1	**Create Webinar Slides**				
4		Draft webinar slide outline		25-Jun		
5		Draft slides		1-Jul		
6		Finalize slides		6-Jul		
7		Email slides to ABC Global Fioundation for comment		6-Jul		
8	Week 2	**Create Landing Pages**				
9		Create subscribe landing page		9-Jul		
10		Create download landing page		9-Jul		
11		Create registration widget		9-Jul		
12		Test landing pages		9-Jul		
13	Week 3	**Do Webinar Run-through**				
14		Do webinar run-through		10-Jul		
15		Record feedback		10-Jul		
16		Adjust slide content accordingly				
17	Week 4	**Do Webinar**				
18		Present webinar		24-Jul		
19		Email ABC Global Foundation for statistics		24-Jul		
20	Week 5	**LinkedIn Email Campaign**				
21		Export email addresses from Linkedin		30-Jul		
22		Upload addresses to MailChimp		30-Jul		
23		Send out emails		31-Jul		
24		Track report statistics		31-Jul		

Download at:
ministryTHRIVE.com/IYE/ActionPlanScheduleExample.xlsx

Ignite Your Email Campaign

Action Plan Schedule Worksheet

	A	B	C	D	E	F
1			**Action Plan Schedule Example**			
2	Date	Task	Person	Deadline	Actual	Comments
3	Week 1	Task				
4						
5						
6						
7						
8	Week 2	Task				
9						
10						
11						
12						
13	Week 3	Task				
14						
15						
16						
17						
18	Week 4	Task				
19						
20						
21						
22						
23	Week 5	Task				
24						
25						
26						
27						

Download at:
ministryTHRIVE.com/IYE/ActionPlanScheduleWorksheet.xlsx

Chapter 6...

Readying the Team
(5 MIN READ)

J im Collins, in his best-selling book, Good to Great, relates the importance of hiring the right people in an organization with seating people in just the right seats on a bus. Assigning everyone the right tasks in an email campaign is just as important.

If we think about the four talents needed to pull off a successful email campaign we have the: *writer, marketer, technician,* and *monitor,* one person may not be suited for the demands of all four positions. Think about asking for help.

Let's look at the four different contributors:

The Writer

If you do not like to write, composing content for email campaigns may be seen as a real drudge.

Writing is a skill that can be learned over time. There are endless resources at the local bookstores and online. Learn from those that have gone before.

> *"If you do not like to write, composing content for email campaigns may be seen as a real struggle."*

Here are five ingredients that will help you write more interesting emails:

- **Curiosity** – Is the headline interesting? Does the story start out with a great hook? Does it pique the reader's curiosity? Does what you're writing about draw the reader into the story? You need to use images that help tell the story and relate well to the content. Use people in photos at every opportunity.

- **Urgency** – Does what you're writing about create a sense of urgency? Why are you writing now? What's happening? What's going to happen if people do not join in? Timing is everything. If you're asking people to read what was sent, what is it you want them to do?

- **Relevance** – The question you have to answer when writing a piece is why do people care about this? How does what's written line up with what they are passionate about? Everyone may not feel the same way about everything you have to say. You need to tap into their passion and interest in what you're trying to accomplish.

- **Value** – Does what's written deliver value? Will the reader's life be any different after reading your piece? Will they know more about an issue? Will they be closer to deciding about donating or joining the cause? Will what's written stir them to act?

- **Emotion** – Sharing what you care about will likely invoke the reader's passion as well. Talk about why you're doing what you're doing. Don't just share the what, when, and how. People want to know what makes you expend so much energy to see a problem eliminated. Honesty breeds trust and trust is a big component in people deciding the cause is worth supporting.

The Marketer

It's the marketer's job to make sure the right message goes out to the right audience. It's that person's mission to fine-tune the content and make it: interesting, relevant, timely, and action-driven.

This person works at making sure the content is passionate and results-driven.

The Technician

The technician drives the email campaign. He or she is responsible for employing the email campaign technology necessary to achieve the best results. Programs such as MailChimp.com, iContact.com, and ConstantContact.com do a great job of providing tutorials, examples, and templates so that almost anyone with little or no previous experience can become an email campaign rock star.

Take the time to explore the top email automation providers and chose the one that's most comfortable.

The Monitor

Tip: The person monitoring the campaigns must be able to draw a distinction between the metrics that are interesting numbers and those that are most important.

Yes, it's important to know how many people are opening the email and how many click-through to the landing page with the offer. But those numbers are secondary to how many people either: join, subscribe, volunteer, or donate.

Tip: Stay focused on the numbers that are most meaningful in relation to the stated goals.

Granted, you may be acting as chief cook and bottle washer in your single-person operation. If that's the case, and you feel uncomfortable handling all the responsibilities of running an email campaign, then perhaps forming an advisory team to help is the perfect solution.

Aside from forming an advisory team, contractors can be hired, or interns could be brought on board. There may even be friends or colleagues that can be enlisted.

Going it alone will be difficult, but not impossible.

Chapter 7...

Executing the Plan
(4 MIN READ)

Here are four elements that help ensure the plan that is prepared runs to a successful conclusion and meets or succeeds the organization's expectations. It's important that someone continually **restate the priorities** so everyone on the team understands what's most crucial. If team members have varying opinions of what's central, they will begin to work against each other. Keep close tabs on the **data collection**. It will be impossible to measure the progress, or success, of the email campaigns if the data is mishandled. The collected data will also be used later on in the process to adjust the campaign to fine-tune things to gain the best results. **Continuous communication** ensures everyone will be on the same page. Each member must understand the goals, and direction of the campaigns. Frequent interactions with team members safeguard against problems scuttling the success. Make sure the email campaign **strategy itself is periodically evaluated** to guarantee the best possible outcome. The landscape may begin to shift as the campaign unfolds. If that's the case, the strategy may need adjustment. Periodic reviews also give the team time to evaluate the original strategy to see if even more progress is possible.

Plans are usually comprised of the Five Ws: Who, What, When, Where, and Why. Let's throw an "H" in for How.

- Who was involved?
- What happened?
- When did it take place?
- Where did it take place?
- Why did it happen?
- How did it happen?

Who Was Involved?

In the previous chapter, four participants were identified: The Writer, The Marketer, The Technician, and The Monitor. The Writer is responsible for drafting the messages. The Marker makes sure the messages are relevant, compelling, and action-driven. The Technician works to make sure the email campaigns run smoothly. The Monitor analyzes the campaign data and reports back to the team.

What Happened?

The email campaign itself is "the What." Suppose we have an educational site that trains pastors on how to plant churches. Upon signing up for the 30-day free trial we decide to send out a series of eight emails over 17 days welcoming the potential students. Here's what the email campaign might resemble:

- Email 1. Sent out upon registering for the free training. This email confirms their sign-up.
- Email 2. Sent out on Day 1. Welcomes the student.
- Email 3. Sent out on Day 3. Focuses on a major feature that benefits the student.
- Email 4. Sent out on Day 7. Focuses on a second major feature.
- Email 5. Sent out on Day 11. Focuses on a third major feature.
- Email 6. Sent out on Day 13. Focuses on a fourth major feature.
- Email 7. Sent out on Day 15. Let's the student know the free trial is expiring.
- Email 8. Sent out on Day 17. Makes the student aware of a special offer if he or she enrolls.

This email campaign strategy is nonthreatening because the potential student can opt-out at any time. The emails keep the person engaged with compelling information about some of the important benefit-driven features of the educational product. At the end of the trial, people can either register or leave.

When Did It Take Place?

In this example the "What" and the "When" may be hard to separate. The *what* talks about the type of email message being sent to the recipients. The *when* focuses on the timing and frequency—the day, the time, and how often.

Where Did It Take Place?

The *where* becomes obvious. The email campaign is taking place online with the aid of an email automation program such as MailChimp.com. Mystery solved.

Why Did It happen?

Why is this happening relates back to our goals. Imagine our goal for this email campaign for the next 30 days is to acquire 100 new pastors who are interested in church planting.

How Did It Happen?

How tells the story of whether the email campaign was successful. Did we reach the stated goals?

Chapter 8...

Monitoring and Learning
(4 MIN READ)

Blasting email messages out to donors and potential supporters and hoping for the best is really pointless. Without the aid of a program such as MailChimp.com or ConstantContact.com, how will a person know how many emails were opened, who clicked on the links within the messages, how many people never want to hear from us again, or which message performed best?

With an email automation tool such as MailChimp.com, we can monitor what's going on, we can learn what's working and what's not performing well. Programs like MailChimp.com help one understand what changes need to be made to have better success at reaching people.

Let's look back at a snapshot of a MailChimp.com report we saw earlier to see what we can learn.

Open rate		43.6%	Click rate		12%
List avg		35.1%	List avg		7.4%
Industry avg		19.4%	Industry avg		1.6%
4,969	**1,368**		**17**		**2**
Opened	Clicked		Bounced		Unsubscribed

The open-rate for this campaign is 43.6%. The national average for the non-profit sector is 19.4%. The open-rate for this campaign is nearing an open-rate three times the national average. We can at least come to two assumptions: first, this was a very successful campaign and second, it's likely this organization emailed its recipients on a consistent basis in the past.

The click-through rate bears out the same facts. It's almost eight times as successful. The high click-through rate also eludes to the fact the email was likely compelling and the offer was seen as valuable.

The bounce rate was low as were the unsubscribes. Watch the unsubscribe rate, it's a good indication people no longer want to hear from us or they do not want to hear from us as often.

> *"The unsubscribe rate is a good barometer for how many and how often we should send people email messages."*

Here's one more MailChimp.com report snippet:

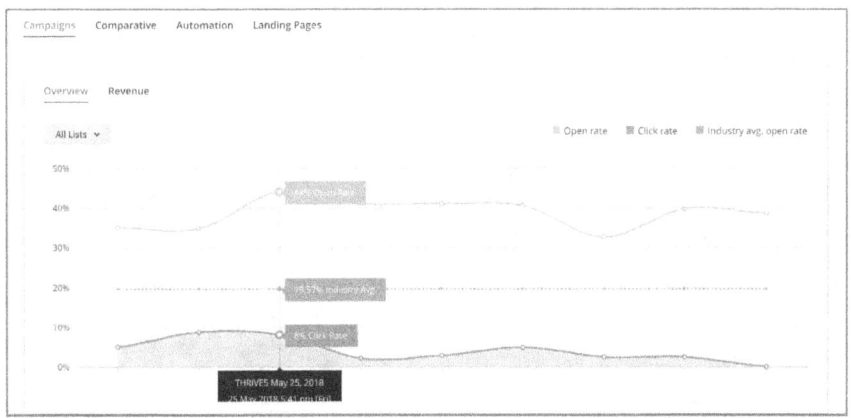

In this example, we can see the last eight email campaigns. We can also see which ones were more successful than the others. For instance, the May 25, 2018 campaign was the most successful with an open-rate of 44% and a click-through rate of 8.8%. This is a great historical graph when needing an overview of what's transpired over a certain period of time.

Tip: Without ways to monitor what's happening, we'll be unable to learn from what's taking place.

Chapter 9...

Testing and Adapting
(5 MIN READ)

If the email campaign under preforms, it will not be immediately obvious which parts are working well and which parts are preforming poorly. Some diagnostics need to be done to uncover the culprits that are keeping us from achieving our goals.

Suppose we look at a list of potential guilty parties:

- The email could have been sent out on the wrong day or at an inconvenient time
- Perhaps the Subject line was unappealing
- The content may not have been compelling enough
- The offer was not seen as having real value

- Recipients did not recognize the sender
- The content was too long and seen as a time-consuming read
- The content was not relevant
- The email format looked unprofessional
- The message and audience did not match up
- Obvious spelling mistakes put people off
- Recipients did not understand the purpose of the message
- The call-to-action was unclear
- There was no call-to-action
- The email was seen as SPAM
- The message was not personalized

As we can see, there are loads of reasons email campaigns can get off track. It's important to identify what's not working correctly so things can be fixed.

Tip: Two skills are vital when diagnosing a problem. First, never eliminate a suspect until the problem has been identified and second, change one thing at a time so the real problem area can be spotted.

Let's go through some examples.

Suppose we suspect the day and time we sent out the emails is the reason for the low open-rate. Let's further suppose we have 1,000 addresses in our contact file. We could divide the list into three groups and send out three emails on three different days to see which day preforms best.

If we suspect the Subject line is the weak point, we could send out three emails with different Subject lines to see which message garners the best results.

Just remember to change one thing at a time and test the theories fully.

> *"Just remember to change one thing at a time and test the theories fully."*

Many of the email automation platforms like MailChimp.com have A/B testing facilities to make uncovering the problem areas easier.

Adapting means you won't settle for the *status quo*. If things are not working, then changes need to be made. For example, suppose the open-rate is extremely low. That could mean several issues are at play. The timing may not be the best. Low open-rates are usually symptomatic of emails that are not welcomed, or the Subject line is not interesting or compelling.

If people are opening the email but not acting, it could mean the message is not compelling or action-driven.

Tip: If the recipients receiving the message are not clicking on the offer, perhaps it is not seen as having value.

Ignite Your Email Campaign

Action Plan Schedule Example

	A	B	C	D	E	F
1			Action Plan Schedule Example			
2	July '18	Task	Person	Deadline	Actual	Comments
3	Week 1	**Create Webinar Slides**				
4		Draft webinar slide outline		25-Jun		
5		Draft slides		1-Jul		
6		Finalize slides		6-Jul		
7		Email slides to ABC Global Floundation for comment		6-Jul		
8	Week 2	**Create Landing Pages**				
9		Create subscribe landing page		9-Jul		
10		Create download landing page		9-Jul		
11		Create registration widget		9-Jul		
12		Test landing pages		9-Jul		
13	Week 3	**Do Webinar Run-through**				
14		Do webinar run-through		10-Jul		
15		Record feedback		10-Jul		
16		Adjust slide content accordingly				
17	Week 4	**Do Webinar**				
18		Present webinar		24-Jul		
19		Email ABC Global Foundation for statistics		24-Jul		
20	Week 5	**LinkedIn Email Campaign**				
21		Export email addresses from LinkedIn		30-Jul		
22		Upload addresses to MailChimp		30-Jul		
23		Send out emails		31-Jul		
24		Track report statistics		31-Jul		

Download at:
ministryTHRIVE.com/IYE/ActionPlanScheduleExample.xlsx

Ignite Your Email Campaign

Action Plan Schedule Worksheet

	A	B	C	D	E	F
1			Action Plan Schedule Example			
2	Date	Task	Person	Deadline	Actual	Comments
3	Week 1	Task				
4						
5						
6						
7						
8	Week 2	Task				
9						
10						
11						
12						
13	Week 3	Task				
14						
15						
16						
17						
18	Week 4	Task				
19						
20						
21						
22						
23	Week 5	Task				
24						
25						
26						
27						

Download at:
ministryTHRIVE.com/IYE/ActionPlanScheduleWorksheet.xlsx

PART III

Writing Action-driven Content

Chapter 10...

Writing with a Purpose
(11 MIN READ)

Before sharing news, ask yourself these two questions, "*Why am I sharing this news?*" and "*Will the reader care about what I have to say?*"

In *Ignite Your Donor Passion*, (available on Amazon.com) I list a variety of purposeful reasons why one might communicate with a small or large group of constituents or potential donors. Following is a portion of that list:

Deliver a Professional Look-and-feel

Remember, handing a person a business card or brochure or sending them an email, newsletter, or speaking out on social media needs to instill a person's confidence and trust in the organization.

It's quite likely that one may never personally meet many of the organization's potential supporters. So, the material initially sent out represents the organization's first impression. Here are some thoughts to consider when building the organization's professional look-and-feel:

- Have a professional design the materials for the organization (logo, business card, brochure, website.) Skip the brother-in-law or neighbor-down-the-street connection. How many of us would opt to go under the knife of the cheapest brain surgeon in town?

> **Did you know?**
> According to *web credibility research* from Stanford, **75%** of users admit to making judgements about an organization based on their web design.

- Be sure all the materials have what is called a "family-look." In other words, use the same colors with the same font styles. The materials, spread out on a table, should look as if they have all come from the same organization.

- Make sure to use good photography. Pictures that tell great stories. Images that load fast on the website and mobile devices. Images that are slow to load cause visitors to go elsewhere. Use images that are readable no matter where they appear. It does little good to show someone a picture the size of a postage stamp.

- Spelling and grammar checking go without saying. Find someone to proof everything before it goes out or that is published to the web.
- Make sure the information being conveyed is not only well-thought out but also well laid out.

- Always leave some open real estate (white space) whether designing a brochure, newsletter, or web page. Not every square inch needs to be crowded with text and images.

Be Seen in All the Right Places

The shotgun approach to looking for potential donors or supporters just won't work on the web; it's too enormous. To be successful here, organizations need to identify their ideal prospects first and then develop, launch, and execute their engagement campaigns.

With the ideal prospects known and their possible watering holes marked off, the next chore is to develop strategies to gain visibility in those venues. Too many organizations are enraptured with the idea of attracting their first 1 million visitors to their own website.

Having good visibility, compelling stories, and attractive offers will attract those people in droves.

"Efficiency is doing things right; effectiveness is doing the right things."
—Peter Drucker

Don't Post the Same Content

Don't post the same content on all your channels. People are bound to see you in more than one place. If they see the same information they'll get bored and stop reading what you have to say.

Besides, people expect to converse differently on the various channels. LinkedIn is more serious, more business-like. Facebook is friendlier, more like attending a block party. Twitter is more akin to walking through a crowded room where people are talking about a particular subject. Come back 10 minutes later and the conversation will have shifted to another topic.

Think about posting an article on your blog. Then chopping it up into a few good sentences or paragraphs and post those on Facebook. Next, choose a few nuggets of wisdom and put them up on Twitter. Instagram would be the perfect place to post pictures on the subject if they're available. At each location, make sure to give the content a soft edit so the information sounds slightly different.

Focus on the Donor

Avoid using words such as "I", "me", "my", "we", or "us." These words tend to remove the reader from the story. Write with a donor-centric approach. Here's an example:

"We worked hard and now we have built a new dormitory for our girls."

Vs.

"Because of your generosity and others, the girls can now enjoy their new, 20-bed dormitory."

The first sentence focuses on the organization. The organization was obviously involved. But, the sentence leaves the donor's contribution out of the picture. The second sentence outlines what was accomplished because of the donor's support.

Whether sending out an email, support letter, or writing a blog post, keep the spotlight on the donor's involvement. Write as if they are an active part of the team—even if the work is being done thousands of miles away.

Relate to the Reader

Drop the "church-speak" or "ministry mumbo jumbo". Write in plain, simple language people understand. Using words or expressions supporters are unfamiliar with make readers uncomfortable. They may not be onboard with the latest terminology or how things are explained in foreign cultures, and therefore feel left in the dark.

 It's important to tune the writing to the readership.

It may be advantageous to use certain terms. If that's the case, then bring people along slowly by explaining the use of the words or phrase the first time they appear.

Timing is Everything

Timing always has been and always will mean "everything." End-of-the-year support letters cannot be sent out the last week of December with the expectation they will be enormously successful. Newsletters cannot be sent out randomly or on a haphazard schedule. Replies on social media need to be almost immediate.

Each organization needs to find the times that work best for their supporters and their team members. If a newsletter is being sent out, do more people read the publication if it's delivered in the morning or the afternoon? Do more readers open the email at the beginning of the month or at the end? Are the supporters more involved in social media between the hours of 9 AM and 11 AM or between 3 PM and 5 PM? Are the phone calls more successful during the week or on weekends?

Take the time necessary to discover the best times to send out the various materials you use to communicate and engage with your potential supporters and donors.

Stay Consistent

Consistency is closely tied to *"Timing is Everything."* Once the organization determines the best times to communicate and engage their supporters it's important to stick with those times. There are, of course, always exceptions that may vary a schedule. Make sure the reason makes sense to all those involved.

If the organization has several irons in the fire, such as: sending out monthly newsletters along with occasional emails, while posting on a blog, and engaging in social media, make sure the timing of all the activities do not overburden the team.

Don't over commit. Start out slowly and ramp things up as success is shown.

Meet on Common Ground

Be sensitive enough to understand how people want to engage with the organization. Younger audiences prefer communicating on social media in short bursts. They'll prefer watching a video instead of reading a three-page newsletter. They're on Facebook, Instagram, and Snapchat. The more veteran crowd enjoys reading and wouldn't mind receiving a newsletter by email. Some still prefer receiving their information by US Mail.

 Synchronize the communication methods to the preferences of the intended audience.

Trumpet Your Value Proposition

An organization's value proposition, or uniqueness, should be obvious, concise, understandable, and evident in all its communications. Don't be too proud to shout it from the rooftops.

It answers the one question on every potential donor's mind,

"Why should I give to this organization instead of some other worthy cause?"

Kissmetrics.com has a sound definition for Value Proposition: A believable collection of the most persuasive reasons people should notice you and take the action you're asking."

Here are a few you might be familiar with:

> Walmart – Save Money Live Better
> Apple – The Experience IS the Product
> Uber – The Smartest Way to Get Around
> Young Life – You Were Made for This
> Navigators – Disciples Making Disciples
> Project:Caleb – Connecting People to Jesus

Cause Less Friction

People make numerous minor decisions before they make a major one. Think about the thought process one goes through when receiving an email.

- The message hits the in-box and your MacBook chirps its arrival.
- You glance at the Sender's name.
- Decide if you have the time to look further.

- Maybe the Subject line interests you, perhaps not.
- You open the message.
- Now you quickly read the first half sentence or so.
- Again, you decide whether to proceed or not.
- You decide you have a moment and read on.
- Half way through the email you conclude it's not urgent and does not require a quick reply.
- It's back to work.

> **Did you know?**
> A radical redesign that reduces friction and increases the force of the value proposition affects donor conversion by **134%**. (NextAfter.com Experiment #5729)

Think of how this process is magnified once you decide to click on the link within the email and head to the donation page. Most of the initial ten decisions are made once again. And if you do decide to give a gift to the organization there are all those personal banking questions one must contemplate giving before hitting the DONATE button.

A person might make dozens of minor decisions before gifting $25 to an organization.

Each decision causes some level of friction. The more the friction the better chance the person will leave the donation process before hitting the DONATE button.

Friction Meter

What's causing the friction is the struggle between **value** and **cost**. Does what the person is being asked to do cost them more than the perceived value of what they'll gain?

Think of asking a person for their email address and giving them nothing in return. The person is asked to give up their email address (value) for nothing in exchange (cost). The friction here is intolerable. Few, if any, people would give their email address to an organization for nothing in return.

Here's another example. Think of asking a person for their postal address, phone number, and email address as opposed to just asking for their email. The friction generated by asking for all three pieces of personal information is huge.

People can only assume if they give someone their phone number they'll start receiving calls—unsolicited, unwanted, unwelcomed calls during the diner hour. If one gives an organization their postal address is it reasonable for them to assume they will shortly be receiving junk mail?

It cannot be overstated that the email sent out, the donation page people are routed to, and the donation form itself that captures a person's information must be finely tuned. Free of any distractions. Free of any unnecessary hoops people should jump through. The donation form needs to ask only for the needed information to process the gift and nothing more.

 **Making the gifting process more difficult than it needs to be only builds friction—and friction leads to rejection.**

 Make sure the value out-weights the cost.

Say It Impactfully

Saying things with impact takes some artful writing. Some of those tools you thought not very useful during high school English class finally come into play.

Writing impactfully requires the use of action words and action verbs. If you're stuck on what words to use, browse the Internet looking for "positive" or "action" words or verbs—there are hundreds.

Writing impactfully requires the message be written in *active* not *passive* voice. Remember, *active voice* describes a sentence where the subject performs the action stated by the verb. In *passive voice* sentences, the subject is acted upon by the verb.

Bob posted the video on Facebook. (active voice)
The video was posted on Facebook by Bob. (passive voice)

Sell the story with headlines that grab the reader's attention.

 Write with emotion.

Make the story sound like it's coming from a human being. Be real. Be authentic.

Convince the reader why he or she should care. Don't focus on just a few members in the readership audience. Take a broad approach when writing. Try to include as many readers as possible.

> *"Readers tend to remember 100% of what they've read when the sentences average eight words or less."*

Focus on what the audience most wants to hear. This means the writer must know his or her audience well. Don't lump everyone into one general, non-descript assemblage.

Call Donors to Action

Think of a call-to-action as a conversion device. Calls-to-action require a higher level of commitment. These mechanisms also serve to move the potential supporter further along in the decision-making process.

> **Did you know?**
> Increased authority and an active call-to-action produced a **64%** surge in downstream conversions.
> (NextAfter.com Experiment #7844)

The call-to-action might be asking visitors to subscribe to a free, monthly newsletter or receive a free eBook.

Keep in mind that it is just as important to have a strategy that deals with what happens after the visitor makes the decision. What takes place after they sign up for the free webinar or download the free eBook.

Create urgency in the mind of the recipient by giving the call-to-action an expiration date, real or imaginary.

Do not use motion, a smiling face, a waving hand, or a bouncing arrow in the call-to-action. It only distracts the visitor.

Segment Your Audience

Once the mechanisms are in place to collect email addresses, the next task is to divide the audience into what are called *personas*.

Per•son•a – the aspect of someone's character that is presented to or perceived by others.

Let's think about assigning *personas* to volunteers, team or board members, potential donors, and regular givers. You may even want to divide up donors into categories such as one-time givers, monthly donors, and major donors.

We'll want to assign *personas* to our donor file because one size does not fit all. It's important to send out personalized, meaningful messages to each group.

Some supporters give on a regular basis, others monthly, and still others when a crisis arises. Certain people give more than others. There are individuals who want to know in more detail about what's happening. Some want to be engaged more than others. Some may offer to volunteer, others won't. Some are interested in the spiritual-wellbeing, while still others may be attentive to the construction or environmental projects. Some want to hear from you on quite a regular basis while others may think hearing from you every month or so works fine.

To achieve the right balance when sending out email messages with the right topics to the correct audience, the overall group needs to be segmented. The sender also needs to be tuned into each donor's passion.

There are times when only current donors need to receive the message. Then times when potential givers need to be educated and encouraged to join the cause.

The delineation between *personas* can be simple or complex. If the system designed achieves the goal of sending the right message to the right group, at the right time, and in the right way, then all's fine.

Share Great Content

When you read a good book, come across a blog that's useful or listen to a podcast or view a video that imparts wisdom your audience would love to hear—share it.

People will appreciate that fact that you're watching out for their best interests.

Sharing other people's thoughts will also help bolster your position on a particular subject.

Leave insecurity behind.

Boosting Donor Generosity

There are a variety of ways to boost donor generosity. You'll have to decide on the ones that you believe work best for the organization.

- Give your donors bragging rights. Consistently tell your supporters their generosity is the reason the work is progressing so well.

- Ask your donors for support on a regular basis. Forget the one, awkwardly-written appeal letter the week before Christmas.

- Make your donors aware of the various giving options the organization offers.

- Let donors know that organizations run smoother when they're able to budget expenses. Encourage your supporters to give by way of monthly electronic payments (ACH).

"Make your donors aware of the various giving options the organization offers."

- This may be a no-brainer but make giving to the organization as easy as possible. Remove any impediments from the payment process.

- Think about having a special giving day such as GivingTuesday (the Tuesday after Thanksgiving Day.)

- Make sure donors understand the scope and size of your vision for the coming year and beyond.

- Don't assume people know how to be biblical stewards. Perhaps sending them a study on the subject would be helpful.

- Always talk about the impact the work is making and how people's lives are being changed.

- Keep your most committed donors happy and well-informed.

- Tell stories that tap into people's empathy.

- Ask them to volunteer. Ask for their advice or ideas.

- Share solid results. Donors want to trust their funds are being used wisely.

- Focus on the "why" more and less on the "what" and "how." For example, it's good for people to know the new dormitory opens next month and that there are 30 new beds available. It's good for them to know it's a cinderblock building with a metal roof with five windows per side. It's also good to know that a sponsor family will be housed with the children. But keep the focus on how the children's lives will be changed as a result of the new dormitory. The children will be well-cared for, safer, in a cleaner environment. Looked after by a loving couple. They'll be happier. Highlight what the children are learning because of being under the watchful eye of loving, Christian care-givers.

Expressing Urgency

Let donors know on some regular basis how things are progressing whether the need is spiritual, financial, emotional, or related to some construction schedule that has fallen behind.

No one deals well with surprises.

Put together a schedule to keep donors informed. Perhaps spiritual requests can go out monthly but also when a dire situation arises. The balance of the information could be put in a scheduled newsletter that goes out on a regular basis.

Being Blatantly Honest

Don't hide the fact or be embarrassed that the fundraising efforts are behind. Many support letters include, in very small print, sometimes in gray lettering, at the very bottom of the letter, a sentence that resembles this example:

> To support our ministry, click here. Thank you.

 Tip: Organizations need to be unabashedly honest with their supporters.

If the goal is to raise $2,200 a month, and one finds him or herself $1,500 behind for the month, how will supporters know or understand how dire the situation is that exists?

Closing the Gap

It's 6,638 miles from Colorado Springs, Colorado to Ghana, West Africa. Ghana is dry in the winter and hot and rainy in the summer. The monsoon season lasts from May to September. Most of the roads are unpaved and you won't find a Starbucks at every busy intersection. Things are very different. The people are different. The environment is different. The business sectors are different. The political climate is different.

Tip: It's important to close the gap between the donor and where the work is being done.

Write some pieces that feature the differences between the two geographic areas. Weave bits of information within the stories you tell. Help the potential supporters and donors understand and see the breath and scope of what the people being helped are facing.

Stay Results Orientated

Donors want to know they've made a wise investment in the organization's work. They want to be reassured the funds are making the most impact possible.

Publish regular reports on the progress being made and the impact being realized. The reports can be a simple paragraph letting the supporters know all is well—the projects are on time and on budget. Better yet, would be the announcement that things are ahead of schedule and under budget.

Sharing Personal Information

Give readers a peak behind the curtain. Share details of your personal life or behind the scenes of the organization. Let people know you're real and that you are dealing with life's ups and downs just as they are.

Sharing personal information helps strengthen the relationship between writer and reader.

Let the readers know how the successes and struggles of the organization affect you on a personal level.

> **"Sharing personal information helps strengthen the relationship between writer and reader."**

If appropriate, share family details as well.

The more the writer and reader have in common the stronger the bond becomes.

Communicating Impact

Saying things with impact takes some artful writing. Some of those tools you thought not very useful during high school English class finally come into play.

Writing impactfully requires the use of action words and action verbs. If you're stuck on what words to use, browse the Internet looking for "positive" or "action" words or verbs—there are hundreds.

Tip: Impactful writing requires the message be written in *active* not *passive* voice.

Remember, *active voice* describes a sentence where the subject performs the action stated by the verb. In *passive voice* sentences, the subject is acted upon by the verb.

Bob posted the video on Facebook. (active voice)
The video was posted on Facebook by Bob. (passive voice)

 Tip: Sell the story with headlines that grab the reader's attention.

Informing

If the purpose is to **inform** potential supporters or donors about what's happening on the ground, be specific. Share as many details as you believe prudent and relevant to the story.

If fundraising has been less than stellar during the past year, be honest with your donors in laying out where you are financially today and where you need to be to continue the work. Give them something precise to pray about or to support.

Educating

If the purpose of the message is to **educate** people about raising up local pastors and planting churches in Ghana in the subregion of West Africa, perhaps this might be a good educational angle:

First, you need to close the geographic gap that exists between Ghana and the US. The distance between the city of Colorado Springs and Kumasi, Ghana is 6,638 miles. That's a long way for someone unfamiliar with the region to guess what situations people are living with each day. Next, people need to understand the work in terms of the needed resources and timing. Let the reader know there are seven cities you hope to reach over the next three years. That raising up five pastors and planting the first home groups takes six to nine months. Then, highlight the necessary resources and finances necessary. From there those that read the email will understand the organization's vision and the amount of hard work ahead of the team.

Engaging

In writing emails that *engage*, grab the reader's attention at once. Tell a great story. Write in short sentences. Use active voice. Ask open-ended or though-provoking questions. Use POWERFUL words that connect with the reader. Write expecting the reader to respond back—be prepared to answer the inquiries or comments promptly.

> "Write expecting the reader to respond back—be prepared to answer the inquiries or comments promptly."

 Engagement requires action by both parties. The communication should not flow in only one direction.

Inspiring

Inspiring the reader takes preparation and thought. Words cannot just be thrown down on paper.

Use pictures or photos that show the work in action. Showcase the impact being made by the organization.

 Tip: Use titles and graphics that help convey emotion.

Write as if you're conversing with a best friend.

Know the audience and understand where their passions lie.

 Tip: If you're still stuck on how to get started, read inspiring communiques by others and learn from those who are having success.

Call-to-Action

Think of a call-to-action as a conversion device. Calls-to-action require a higher level of commitment. These mechanisms also serve to move the potential supporter further along in the decision-making process.

> **Did you know?**
> Increased authority and an active call-to-action produced a **64%** surge in downstream conversions.
> (NextAfter.com Experiment #7844)

The call-to-action might be asking visitors to donate, subscribe to a free, monthly newsletter or receive a free eBook.

 **Tip: Keep in mind that it is just as important to have a strategy that deals with what happens after the visitor makes the decision.**

What takes place after they sign up for the free webinar or download the free eBook?

Create urgency in the mind of the recipient by giving the call-to-action an expiration date, real or imaginary.

> **Did you know?**
> Whole Whale is predicting **$201 million** will be raised this #GivingTuesday a **20%** increase over last year's **$160 million**.

Chapter 11...

Personalizing Your Message
(3 MIN READ)

Let's look at three areas where personalization can make a huge difference in the open-rate. First, we have the sender's name. People like to hear from people so make sure the email sender is a person's name and not the name of the organization. Tinker with the sender's name if the emails have been coming from the president of the organization. The email recipients may not believe the leader of the organization has the time to communicate with them. Perhaps the email should come from the fundraising chairperson or another key person within the organization.

Second, personalizing the recipient's name dramatically improves the open-rate (see example). Make every effort to secure the names of the people that are interested in the organization's work. Forget using Dear Supporter, Dear Friend, Dear Donor, and the rest of the tired lot.

> *"Forget using Dear Supporter, Dear Friend, Dear Donor, and the rest of the tired lot."*

The last factor deals with the signature at the end of the message. Surely, you do not use an image of your signature when sending an email to a friend or family member. Stay personal and just sign off using your first or full name depending on the relationship you have with the person. Maybe add the organization if appropriate.

In this example, you can see this email comes from a real person. The message is also personalized.

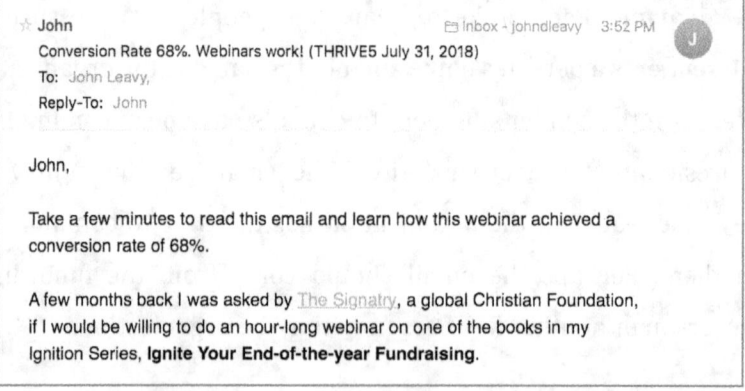

NextAfter.com has run some interesting experiments over the past year or so related to *personalizing emails.*

Experiment #6272 *How including an image in a personal email affects donor conversion* saw an **80.8% lift**.

Experiment #5694 How subject line personalization affects open rate saw a **25.2% lift**.

Experiment #7376 How a more personalized value proposition affects remarketing conversion rate saw a **393.4% lift**.

Experiment #8737 How an individual sender influences email open rates saw a **25.6% lift**.

NextAfter.com is a premier site for experiments like these. Give them a look-see.

Chapter 12...

"Pay No Attention to the Man Behind the Curtain"

(4 MIN READ)

Pay no attention to the man behind the curtain, is a line spoken by The Wizard of Oz, played by Frank Morgan, in the film The Wizard of Oz, directed by Victor Fleming (1939). The Wizard was reluctant to reveal his *true self* to Dorothy and the gang.

Don't take the same posture. Let the readership see your personal side. Let them get to know the *real* you.

Let's review some ideas for sharing yourself with your email recipients. These techniques transfer well to blogging and social media as well. But, we'll stick with using these practices during email campaigns.

Items of Interest

Some writers start out their emails by mentioning what's going on in the world around them. They might mention an upcoming holiday, the weather, a news item everyone is likely thinking about, or an economic happening many people might be facing. It's safe to say, politics and government issues are off the table unless the writer believes his or her recipients have a vested interest in the outcome.

Pick a Focus

Some writers pick a focus to write about as a backdrop for their email campaigns. The ancillary subject matter might be mentioning a country, a culture, or a sport. They might talk about food from a certain country or use cycling terms the readers would be familiar with hearing. This method is a great way to build a secondary relational-bridge between writer and reader.

Discard Grammar Rules

Don't let your high school English teacher read your stuff. Use sentence fragments, mishandle punctuation, start sentences with conjunctions, celebrate incorrect usage by using "like" instead of "such" and don't forget to throw a preposition at the end of a few sentences.

We're not talking about being a writer who ignores every rule written in the Chicago Manual of Style. May it never be! Just try to write with a more causal style. Be yourself. Write the way you converse.

Self-deprecation Doesn't Hurt

Find a way to leverage your faults or traits in what your writing. If people think you have a good sense of humor, then let it shine once in a while. If you're the type of person who's over cautious, make fun of that trait on occasion. Let your readership know you're human.

Refer to Yourself

Refer to yourself by using words such as: "my", "me", and "I." Talk about your trials and successes. Let the readers know you're in the same boat. You have gone through the same trials. Temper the use of this style. With over-use, you might be seen as a person having a larger than life ego.

Use a "Branded" Technique

End every email with a penetrating, thought-provoking, open-ended question to get the recipient thinking. Give the readers a reason to anticipate your next message. Use the questions as a bridge between communiques.

Whatever writing style you choose, stick with it. Be authentic. Be you.

> *"Whatever writing style you choose, stick with it. Be authentic. Be you."*

Lasting relationships between organization and donors can be birthed and built during email campaigns.

Don't try to be someone you ain't. If you're not funny, discard the advice that says you must be amusing and entertaining. Write in a comfortable style or you won't last.

Chapter 13…

Staying Donor-focused

(2 MIN READ)

Here, it seems we have several terms that all mean the same thing: donor-focused, donor-centric, and donor-centered. Whichever term you decide on, they all mean only one thing. Building relationships between the organization and its donors is critical.

When searching for "donor centric" on Google, 27,200 pages pop up. There are articles that promise 20 Ways, 10 Ways, 5 Ways, 9 Ways, 3 Ways, and 7 Ways to be Donor-centric.

It will be difficult to keep several dozen ways in mind as you try to build solid, meaningful, long-lasting relationships with your donors.

Let's highlight the ones that are most important and will probably produce the best results:

- Be grateful. Okay, at times, be over grateful.
- Respond promptly no matter the request or occasion.
- Talk more about the impact their participation is making than the organization's progress.
- When communicating, use words such as "you" and "yours" more than "we," "us," and "our."
- Make sure their personal information is correct. There can be no lapses in calling someone by the wrong name.
- Designate the funds so donors believe they have control over how their money is spent.
- Don't treat every donor the same. Those that give more are showing you they want to be more invested in the work.
- Provide ways donors can give their opinion.
- Give donors *real* ways to be more involved beyond giving.

Remember, if you're not talking to your donors on a regular basis some other organization likely is.

Tip: Never forget the question donors ask themselves on a regular basis, *"Why should I give to this organization, instead of some other worthy cause?"*

Chapter 14...

Empowering with Trigger Words
(2 MIN READ)

You have to love this quote from Mark Twain, *"The difference between the right word and the almost right word is the difference between lightning and a lighting bug."*

Trigger words cause action. Trigger words can transform a so-so email message into an engaging, compelling, conversion-making monster.

Here's a quick list of some trigger word examples Brian Clark compiled over at CopyBlogger.com:

Health: *Boost, Cure, Energize, Flush,* and *Vibrant*

Hope: *Bright, Destiny, Empower, Overcome,* and *Undo*

Anger: *Arrogant, Cruel, Greed, Hate,* and *Unscrupulous*

Frustration: *Had enough, Never again, Pointless, Temporary fix,* and *Tired*

Betrayal: *Burned, Conspiracy, Disinformation, Fleece,* and *Swindle*

Revenge: *Avenge, Payback, Reclaim, Turn the Tables,* and *Vindication*

Forbidden: *Banned, Controversial, Exposed, Insider,* and *Taboo*

Powerless: *Agony, Floundering, Helpless, Paralyzed,* and *Surrender*

Passion: *Blissful, Delightful, Jubilant, Rave,* and *Thrilled*

Urgency: *Before you forget, Deadline, Limited, Seize,* and *While it's fresh on your mind*

Triger words cause the reader to act.

Choose your trigger words wisely as you draft the copy. Don't just go through the motions of putting words down on paper.

Remember, you're trying to evoke the reader's emotions by sending the communique in the first place, true?

Chapter 15...

Delivering Value
(4 MIN READ)

When sending out an email campaign, keep in mind you're asking recipients to stop what they're doing to read your message.

Donors and potential supporters are going to judge the value of the communique, before, during, and after they read the message.

The value within the email message needs to stand up to the repeated tests.

Tip: Email recipients will constantly appraise the message as they read it by asking themselves the question, *"Is my time being well spent?"*

Here are some Dos and Don'ts:

DO be personal.
DON'T be unapproachable.

DO treat audience members differently.
DON'T send the same message to everyone.

DO talk about what matters most to your donors.
DON'T push the same fundraising message in every email.

DO offer something of *real* value.
DON'T think perceived value is real value.
(Skip the logoed water bottles and mouse pads.)

DO tell your stories using visual and compelling details.
DON'T send novellas masquerading as urgent email messages.

DO create emotional connections.
DON'T put the readers to sleep.

DO constantly work on improving donor satisfaction.
DON'T grow complacent with donor relationships.

DO write from the donor's perspective.
DON'T write about what matters most to you.

Do work at developing a memorable donor experience.
DON'T take any relationship for granted.

DO ask for your donor's opinions.
DON'T run the organization in a bubble.

DO continually educate your donors.

DON'T assume you're all on the same page.

> *"Remember, people love to invest in success."*

Remember, people love to invest in success. Always talk about impact, give cold, hard statistics on how lives are being changed or improved as a result of the donor's involvement.

No News is NOT Good News

News should not be misconstrued as something where one person is in the know and a second individual is uninformed.

Merriam-Webster defines "news" as a report of recent events, something having a specified influence or effect, or a matter that is newsworthy.

The operative word in that entire definition is "newsworthy."

Does what you're sharing, whether by blog post, newsletter, email, or social media, better inform, educate, or inspire the reader?

Is the "news" informative, relevant, and meaningful?

> *"Once this relationship of trust is broken it may not be repairable."*

Sharing items that are not newsworthy on a regular basis endangers the relationship between the writer and his or her readership. The more "not really news at all" is shared accelerates the likelihood the readership will dismiss the publication as having little or no value and go elsewhere.

Once this relationship of trust is broken it may not be repairable.

Chapter 16...

Skipping the Non-profit Lingo
(2 MIN READ)

The use of acronyms, jargon, and other fundraising, or non-profit terms may quickly lose the other person (the reader) in the conversation.

Every industry has their "insider" language. It seems like no one has the time to speak in full sentences these days. Texting on our smart phones is not helping the situation any.

Does it take so much time to say, "peer-to-peer and not P2P," "Non-profit Organization and not NPO," or "Return on Investment instead of ROI?"

Of course, our government and military have mastered the art of acronymization and taken it to heights no human will ever ascend.

Using terms, the other party in the conversation does not understand or is not familiar with only causes confusion and befuddlement.

Keep in mind, the donor or potential supporter in the conversation may not be up to speed on all aspects of the non-profit and its organizational nuances.

Maintain a level playing field during each conversation.

Long-time donors are likely to know more than one-time givers. Volunteers and board members are sure to know more of what's happening behind the scenes.

 Tip: It all comes down to—knowing your audience.

Chapter 17...

Calling Readers to Act
(4 MIN READ)

We all understand by now that, *"If we build it, they will NOT come."* Visitors will not stop by our website just because they're on the world wide web.

They won't open and read our emails because they receive them in their in-boxes. People will not automatically come to an understanding on their own that people's live are in the balance and they are in desperate need of assistance.

They will need information, education, engagement, nurturing, and a nudge or two from time-to-time before they will make an informed decision to join the cause.

Does this illustration appear at the bottom of the newsletter sent out by your organization?

> To support our ministry, click here. Thank you.

No one has to raise their hand.

Don't hide the obvious reason for sending the email if the organization is trying to raise funds by getting people to act.

It's not hard to understand what ConstantContact is trying to say. Their automated email platform can help drive big results.

How about a few email examples?

Our weekly newsletter THRIVE5 has a variety of calls to action so the reader can pick and choose what interests him or her most.

John

Are You Doing Everything You Can to Acquire New Email Addresses? (THRIVE5 July 3, 2018)

To: John,

Reply-To: John

Need a new idea on how to acquire more new email addresses?

We receive encouraging comments on the examples & worksheets included in our Ignite Series of books. So, we thought why not create a PDF of 10 of the downloads and send an email to perspective subscribers to see how many would jump at the chance to download the free offer.

Here's our Ignite Your Fundraising (Examples & Worksheets).
We tell you how things worked out next week.

Thing One – Ignite Your Email: Our latest offering in the Ignite Series will be out this month. **Ignite Your Email** focuses on: Boosting Cause Awareness, Increasing Donor Acquisition, Building Lasting Relationships, and Raising More Money.

Thing Two – Don't miss our timely blog posts:
ministryTHRIVE.com/blog

Thing Three – Thanks to NextAfter for Experiment #9150. How a More Concise Value Proposition and Brand-aligned Imagery Boosted the Conversion Rate in Facebook Ads by 80.2%.

Thing Four – Our special THRIVE5 article
Write a Purpose Statement That Sets Your Organization Apart.

Thing Five – Interesting places we visited this past week
Joe Garecht, over at the Fundraising Authority, penned a great article on: Why Some Non-profits Always Hit Their Fundraising Goals.
Michael Hyatt's weekly podcast talked about, Stress-free Business Travel. Have you checked out Adobe Stock Images? Just using someone else's intellectual property without permission can be a costly mistake.

See you there.

THRIVEon!
John

Here's the first part of Michael Hyatt's weekly newsletter:

Michael wastes no time in telling the reader his or her next step: "Read the Magazine."

Our friends at NextAfter.com wondered how an end-of-article call-to-action affects donor conversion rate (Experiment: #8983.)

The conversion rate was boosted a whopping **800.9%**.

 Tip: Don't be embarrassed or afraid to make the call-to-action. Let people say "No." Don't say it for them.

PART IV

Delivering and Tracking Your Campaigns

Chapter 18...

Choosing an Email Platform
(4 MIN READ)

If you search the web for email platform comparisons there's a good chance each survey will rank their favorite company first. Let's face it. Everyone has their preference.

The choice of an email campaign platform is really up to each organization based on their needs and the technical abilities of the staff. Use the surveys as a starting point and not as the last word in email platform performance or preference.

It's true the software that is chosen today to send your emails may not be the best solution long term. It seems like no technology solution fits one's needs forever. Keep your ears to the ground as these companies push out improvements.

> *"Remember, what you cannot do today, you may be able to do twice as fast tomorrow."*

MailChimp.com (home page shown here) is a popular email campaign platform and its features fit well with the needs of ministryTHRIVE. The fact that MailChimp.com allows an organization to email its first 2,000 contacts free forever weighed heavily in our initial decision. Their **Pricing** options worked well as we grew. The **Support** and **Learning** sections helped us get up to speed quickly. The **Blog** always has interesting articles. MailChimp.com is always announcing new options in their **What's New** section.

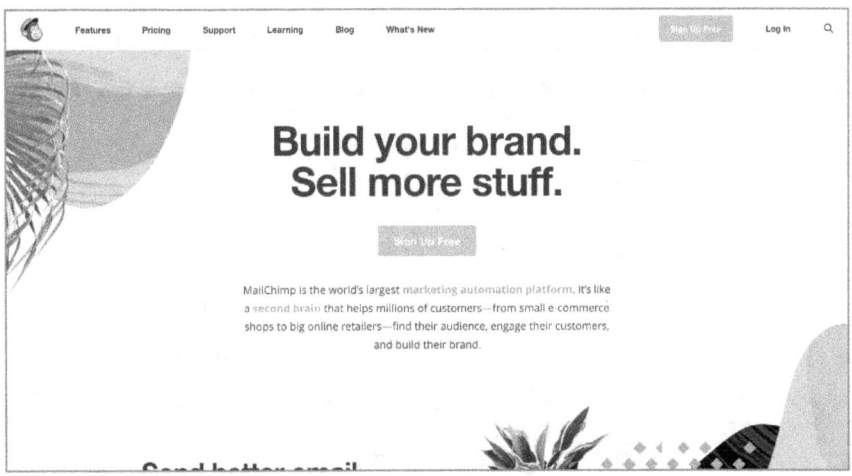

Not sure how to choose the best email platform for your organization? Here's a list of questions to ponder before making your decision:

- Is the service affordable and does it remain cost effective as our contact list and demands grow?
- Is it easy to upload our contact list if it's in a spreadsheet?
- Can we easily add individual contacts as we acquire new email addresses?
- Can we easily segregate our contacts into multiple lists?
- Do they provide email templates, so we can get started quickly?
- Can we upload our own email templates?
- Are their reports easy to understand?
- Do the reports provide information on the key metrics we're most interested in seeing? (open-rate, click-through, bounce, unsubscribes)
- Do they provide a high level of support?
- Do they provide training tutorials?
- Are the email templates and reports mobilized?
- How about their social media integration?
- Do they have good unsubscribe logistics?
- Do they have an anti-spam feature?
- Do they have a landing page creator?
- Do they have an autoresponder feature?
- Do they offer a poll or survey feature?
- Can they help with collecting donations?

- Can we offer coupons through emails?
- Do they offer sign-up forms?

Good luck selecting your platform.

 Tip: Keep in mind, the decision is not carved in stone. You can always move to another platform if the first option turns out to be a bad fit.

Chapter 19...

Uploading Your Contacts
(4 MIN READ)

C reating a list of contacts in any of the email campaign platforms is similar. You answer a few questions to define the list being created and then upload people's contact information.

It makes sense to create several lists when building email campaigns. You might have a list of donors as well as a list of potential supporters. You may even have a list of those people who have subscribed to your weekly newsletter.

Some people might appear in several lists.

Ignite Your Email Campaign

Most platforms let you upload the contacts from a .csv file or by copying and pasting the names from a spreadsheet.

Individual names can be added one-at-a-time later.

Here's what a sample contact spreadsheet might resemble:

	A	B	C	D
1	Don	Aycock	dona@gmail.com	
2	Anthony	Davis	anthonydavis8877@yahoo.com	
3	Sue	Detweiler	sue@detweiler.com	
4	Ron	DiCianni	ron@mail.com	
5	Cynthia	DiTiberio	cdt.editorial@icloud.com	
6	Dr. David	Frisbie	drdavidfrisbie@email.com	
7	Geof	Morin	geof.morin@yahoo.com	
8	Steve	Sammons	ssammons@colorado.edu	
9	Jerry	Wiles	jerry@water.co	
10				

Most platforms let you include the postal address if needed.

When collecting people's personal information, don't ask for more information than you intend to use.

 **Tip: If you only want to send them an email, then only ask for that address. If the need arises later where additional information is needed, then ask for it.**

127 *Chapter 19/Uploading Your Contacts*

Getting Permission

As long as we're talking about sending out e-mails, let's chat about asking the recipient's permission before sending them a message.

Seth Godin wrote a great book in 1999 titled *Permission Marketing*. As a matter of fact, he coined the phrase "permission marketing." Seth's point is that it makes more sense to ask someone's permission to send them something rather than filling their in-box or interrupting their day.

We might say permission marketing is asking our readers to opt-in or subscribe to a newsletter before assuming they want to be added to the circulation database.

> *"Isn't it more reasonable to communicate with dozens of people who want to hear from you than thousands that do not?"*

Isn't it more reasonable to communicate with dozens of people who want to hear from you than thousands that do not?

Double opt-in and GDPR

Here are two terms double opt-in and GDPR, you may not be familiar with, so let's cover them.

You probably didn't know most organizations use a single opt-in feature. This is where the person registering for something, perhaps a newsletter, where they enter their email address into a form and hit Submit. This process is known as single opt-in.

Double opt-in is a three-step process:

1. The person registering for say a newsletter or free offer, enters his or her information and hits Submit.
2. They receive a confirmation email where they must click the confirmation link.
3. Then, their registration information is added to the list of recipients.

GDPR which stands for, General Data Protection Regulation, was instituted by the European Union in 2018. When relying on consent as your legal basis for processing, the GDPR says the consent you obtain must be freely given, specific, informed, and unambiguous. You also must clearly explain how you plan to use the person's information.

 Tip: It is recommended you contact your legal counsel to find out how the GDPR affects you.

Chapter 20...

Creating Your First Campaign
(16 MIN READ)

Email campaigns can play multiple communication roles for an organization. The campaigns might be used to **boost cause awareness, increase name acquisition, build lasting relationships,** or **to raise funds.**

If we take a more-targeted look at these campaigns, we might say they could be enlisted to: announce events, enlist volunteers, launch giveaways, make appeals, send newsletters, share freshly written articles, or inform, educate, and nurture donors and potential supporters.

The emails usually contain hyperlinks, so people can click through to a landing page which collects their information.

Landing pages are integral to email campaigns. A landing page is a web page especially designed for a marketing or advertising campaign. A landing page might be used to collect personal information when soliciting donations. It could be a part of the email campaign to gather people's email addresses or let them register for an event or subscribe to a newsletter.

Here's an example campaign where an email was sent out to see if email recipients would subscribe to a weekly news brief. The bonus for subscribing was a free digital download of, ***Ignite Your Fundraising***. You'll also note two landing pages were used, one to acquire the person's email address and a second page which held the link to the digital eBook.

The email Subject was: Decide before tomorrow. The headline obviously creates a sense of urgency.

The lead sentence confirms the need to respond quickly.

Next, the reader sees the link for the free offer followed by the contents of the new book.

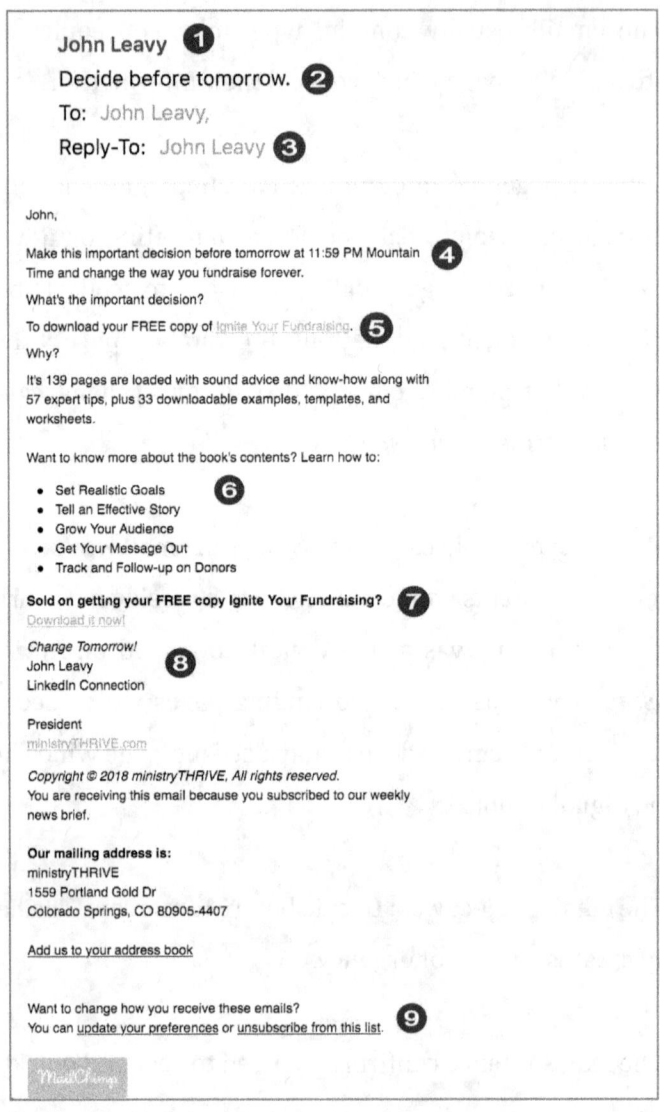

Let's breakdown the structure of the message:

1. **From:** John Leavy – the message is coming from a real person.
2. The **Subject** is brief, succinct, and causes a sense of urgency.
3. **To:, Reply-To:,** and **salutation** are personalized.
4. **The First sentences** – clearly state the purpose of the message.
5. **There is an immediate call-to-action**: To download your FREE copy of *Ignite Your Fundraising*.
6. **Supporting evidence:** sweetens the pot by explaining what the reader will learn by reading the eBook.
7. **A second call-to-action is made:** Download it now!
8. **The valediction or closing:** shows the email came from a real person, not an organization.
9. **Unsubscribe:** the recipient is given the opportunity to unsubscribe or change their preferences for receiving information from the sender.

Now, how about examining the two landing pages?

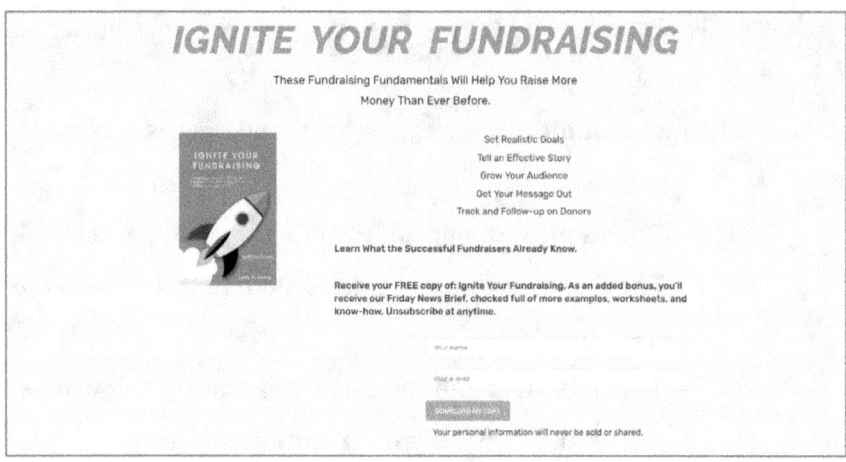

The first landing page captures the person's name and email address. Yes, we already have their name and email address, but they had not yet subscribed to the weekly news brief. This person's contact information will now be loaded into a second file titled, Weekly News Brief.

This landing page provides the download link for the eBook.

Technology could be added to the first landing page where by an email is sent to verify the recipient's email address. That second email would include the download link seen in the second landing page illustration. This practice is used to verify the email address the person enters in the submission form.

How about if we expand our discussion on the anatomy of what goes into a compelling email?

The Anatomy of an Email

The elementary parts of an email message include Sender, Subject, To, Salutation, Copy (or message) and a Signature.

1. **Sender** – People like to hear from people. Forget about using no-reply email addresses. Emailing is a two-way street. People want to be able to respond to the person sending the message. When the recipient sees a "no-reply" sender address he or she will conclude, the person sending the message does not want to hear back from them.

John Leavy

Decide before tomorrow.

To: John Leavy,

Reply-To: John Leavy

John,

Make this important decision before tomorrow at 11:59 PM Mountain Time and change the way you fundraise forever.

What's the important decision?

To download your FREE copy of Ignite Your Fundraising.

Why?

It's 139 pages are loaded with sound advice and know-how along with 57 expert tips, plus 33 downloadable examples, templates, and worksheets.

Want to know more about the book's contents? Learn how to:

- Set Realistic Goals
- Tell an Effective Story
- Grow Your Audience
- Get Your Message Out
- Track and Follow-up on Donors

Sold on getting your FREE copy Ignite Your Fundraising?
Download it now!

Change Tomorrow!
John Leavy
LinkedIn Connection

President
ministryTHRIVE.com

Copyright © 2018 ministryTHRIVE, All rights reserved.
You are receiving this email because you subscribed to our weekly news brief.

Our mailing address is:
ministryTHRIVE
1559 Portland Gold Dr
Colorado Springs, CO 80905-4407

Add us to your address book

Want to change how you receive these emails?
You can update your preferences or unsubscribe from this list.

> **Did you know?**
> **46%** of emails are opened based on the Subject line.

2. **Subject** – DigitalMarketer.com offers eight forms the Subject line might take: Self-interest, Curiosity, Offer, Urgency, Humanity, News, Social Proof, and Story. Let's study an example of each:

Self-interest:

Read about how ministryTHRIVE is changing the face of fundraising.

Curiosity:

More non-profits turn to ministryTHRIVE for fundraising help. Why?

Offer:

Attend a FREE ministryTHRIVE workshop on End-of-the-year Fundraising.

Urgency:

Tomorrow is the last chance to register for the FREE Fundraising Workshop.

Humanity:

Find out how Caring For The Congo is working to rescue 200 orphans in 2018.

News:

Learn how Ghana is becoming the first developed African country by 2029.

Social Proof:

Find out why two million people watched the 2017 Tour De France on mobile devices.

Social Proof: Social proof is the influence that the actions and attitudes of the people around us (either in real life or online) have on our own behavior. The "proof" element is the idea that if other people are doing it (or saying it), it must be correct.

Story:

Did Jack really lack the right stuff for his church's mission trip?

> **Did you know?**
> Personalizing the email can boost the open-rate by **270%**. (NextAfter.com Experiment #5707)

3. **Salutation** – It's time to retire salutations such as: Dear Friend, Dear Supporter, Dear Donor, Trusted Volunteer,

Valued Friend, and the like. What can be more impersonal than not using the name of the person you're writing? Make every effort to record the names, first and last, of each person that crosses your path whether a potential supporter or regular donor. Start the email out by using his or her first name. If you're writing a person for the first time, perhaps using "Dear" before their first name applies. If you intend to send out dozens or hundreds of personalized emails, you'll need to send them out using an email automation marketing system such as MailChimp.com or ConstantContact.com. These systems will merge the person's name into what's being sent out. In this way, each email will go out with the person's name in the salutation.

4. **Message** – Our focus here is on the copy itself and not its intent. When writing copy *less* is always *more*. Say what needs to be said. Say it clearly, be concise, write with passion, and then end the message.

> *"Skip using ALL CAPS, **bold letters** and multiple exclamation points!!!!— say it with words not punctuation."*

5. **Signature** – When sending an email to a friend do you really use an image of your signature,

followed by a bunch of social icons, and a favorite quote or verse-of-the-day? Or do you simply sign off using your first name? The message is going out to a friend, a colleague, an associate. Skip all the templates and branding stuff. Just be yourself.

6. **Attachments** – Unfortunately there are nefarious individuals who use email attachments to spread viruses on unsuspecting recipient's computers. These days, many people will not open an email attachment for that very reason. A better option would be to upload the file, whether a video, newsletter, or whatever to your website and then add a link in the email. People receiving the message with a link are more likely to download the file.

The Anatomy of a Landing Page

The essential components of any effective landing page include: look and feel, headline and subhead, value proposition, benefits, a hero shot, social proof, a supporting statement, closing argument, and a call-to-action.

At times, a few of these components could be combined or are not necessary. For instance, the value proposition or social proof might be included with the image.

1. **Look and feel** – It's vitally important that when the person is routed to the landing page that it has a similar look and feel. The person clicking the hyperlink must feel they're in the right place.

2. **Headline** – In our landing page example the book title is the Headline.

3. **Value Proposition** – The subhead acts as our value proposition.

4. **Benefits Gained from the Book** – Set Realistic Goals, Tell an Effective Story, Grow Your Audience, Get Your Message Out, and Track and Follow-up on Donors.

5. **Hero Shot** – The hero shot of this landing page is an image of our book, ***Ignite Your Fundraising***.

6. **Social Proof** – Social proof is still being developed for this new publication.

7. **Supporting Statement** – Learn What the Successful Fundraisers Already Know acts as our supporting statement.

8. **Closing Argument** – On this landing page we decided to end with a bonus offer (Friday News Brief) instead of a closing argument.

9. **Call-to-action** – The call-to-action is: Download My Copy. Notice the download button is personalized.

Testing 1, 2, 3

Nothing will sabotage an awesome email campaign quicker than spelling or grammar mishaps.

It is important to read and reread the content before launching the email campaign.

Spellchecker is your friend.

Make sure to test all the hyperlinks included in the text and on the landing page.

Once the campaign is ready to go, send a test email to yourself.

Why not send test emails to team or board members as well?

 Tip: You can never have too many eyes looking over the material.

Click on all the links: subscribe, join, and donate. Do whatever it is you're asking the future email recipients to do.

Then look behind the scenes to make sure the information is successfully transferred from the input form to the contact file correctly.

Then and only then, is the campaign ready to roll out.

Send Verses Schedule

Some organizations go with conventional wisdom while others try and avoid it. Conventional wisdom might say the best days to send out emails are: Tuesdays, Wednesdays, and Thursdays. The reasoning goes like this: people are busy starting their week on Mondays and on Fridays, they're trying their hardest to finish out the week.

Sounds reasonable.

Then there are those organizations that rationalize, if everyone else is sending their emails out on Tuesdays, Wednesdays, and Thursday, perhaps we should send ours out on Mondays or Fridays.

The logic here is, people probably receive fewer emails on Mondays and Fridays.

That sounds reasonable as well.

So, what's the answer? Time will tell. Test.

Segment your contact file into several groups and test different days and times until you find the optimal window for sending out your campaigns.

Tip: If you don't have hundreds or thousands of email addresses, choose different days and times to communicate with your audience so see which days and times seem to work best.

Is Your Message Mobilized?

Here are a few sobering statistics every organization had better be aware of: 61% of email opens occur on mobile devices, 75% say they use their smartphones most often to check email, 98% reported they own a mobile device of some kind, and 86% said they access one or more of their email accounts using a mobile device. (courtesy of: Adestra, Fluent, and The Relevance Group) (To the right is a snapshot of the same landing page we were just talking about on a smartphone.)

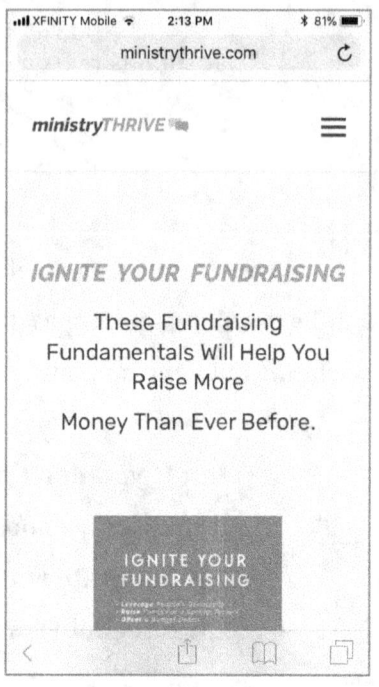

Test reading the emails and landing pages on several devices if possible.

It's a good practice to send the messages to smartphones, tablets, laptops, and desktops.

Chapter 21...

Making Sense of the Reports
(3 MIN READ)

The formatting of the report may differ between email campaign platforms but the basic information we're interested in will be in the basic report.

When running an email campaign, we'll want to know: How many emails were sent out, how many people received the messages successfully, how many email addresses bounced, and how many unsubscribed.

Let's look at a MailChimp.com report snippet from their Knowledge Base:

10 Year Reunion Fundraiser

Overview · Activity · Links · Social · E-commerce · Conversations · Analytics360

6,500 Recipients

List: Independent Donors
Subject: Your 10-Year Reunion is Around the Corner!

Delivered: Wed, Apr 27, 2016 12:00 pm
View email · Download · Print · Share

12	19.95	$239
Orders	Average order revenue	Total revenue

Open rate	51.0%	Click rate	22.3%
List average	51.0%	List average	22.3%
Industry average (Non-Profit)	19.9%	Industry average (Non-Profit)	2.2%

3,316	1,449	0	0
Opened	Clicked	Bounced	Unsubscribed

Successful deliveries	6,500 100.0%	Clicks per unique opens	43.7%
Total opens	4,105	Total clicks	2,680
Last opened	4/27/16 9:00PM	Last clicked	4/27/16 8:01PM
Forwarded	0	Abuse reports	0

From this report we can see that the 10 Year Reunion Fundraiser went out to 6,500 recipients. 12 people placed orders for $19.95 each. The total revenue was $239.

The open-rate was 51% against an industry average of 19.9%. The click-rate was 22.3% over an industry average of 2.2%.

If we focus on opens and click-throughs, the email did amazingly well.

If we drill down a little in the report, the story starts to change.

1,449 people read the copy and decided to click on the offer. The sad news is that only 12 orders were placed. That's a conversion rate of .008%. Something is drastically wrong on the landing page.

These few statistics back up our suspicions. Across industries, the average conversion rate for landing pages is 2.35%. The top 25% of organizations score a conversion rate of 5.31%.

Let's apply these conversion rates to our email campaign to see how well it could have done if the landing page did a better job.

If 2.35% of recipients took the offer, that would mean 340 orders were placed and the campaign would have earned $6,783.

If 5.31% of the recipients took the offer, then 769 orders would have been placed earning $15,341.

As we can see, a few percentage points in one direction or the other means success or failure.

Chapter 22...

Fine-tuning the Campaign
(10 MIN READ)

Email campaigns have more than a few moving parts. At times, it will be difficult to tell what pieces are performing poorly and thereby preventing the organization from reaching its campaign goals.

Fine-tuning the Campaign lists a series of questions, broken down by the chapter headings in this book, to help jog your mind during a postmortem investigative process. Choose the chapter section you believe is causing the problem and run through the questions to see what can be learned.

Once the poor-performing parts are identified, make necessary adjusts before the next campaign launch.

 Tip: Keep in mind, if too many elements of the campaign are changed at the same time, what actually fixed the problem may be clouded.

Review this flight-check list before launching an email campaign:

Achieving Your Goals

- Have safeguards been put in place to avoid against mission-creep?
- Are the goals written down, either electronically or on paper?
- Are the goals: specific, measurable, attainable, realistic, and time-bound?
- Do the goals motivate the team?
- Are the goals in line with the organization's mission?
- Do the goals address the *real* needs of those being served by the organization?
- Are statistical programs in place or is Google Analytics being used?
- Was past historical data available for use in developing the goals?

- Will the goals challenge the team and the donors?
- Are we willing to change the goals if success looks elusive?
- Are intermediate milestones in place to show progress to team members and donors?
- Does everyone on the team understand the priority of the goals?

Preparing the Action Plan

- Have the needed skills been identified?
- Has the timing been set?
- Are the resources ready?
- Has the budget been established?
- Has the plan accounted for the unexpected?
- Have the responsibilities been assigned?
- Has a communication channel been set up?
- Has flexibility been built into the plan?

Readying the Team

- If the team lacks a certain skill what's being done to shore up that deficit?
- Has someone been identified to oversee the team?
- Does every team member have the self-assurance they can complete the assigned tasks?

- Does everyone on the team understand how success has been defined?
- Does each team member understand the problem-escalation process?
- If you're the lone team member, has an advisory team been selected to give constructive criticism of the plan as it unfolds?

Executing the Plan

- Is the data being collected and stored properly?
- Is the strategy being evaluated to ensure success is within reach?
- Is any team member struggling with their assignments?
- Are tasks being completed on time?
- Are the results tracking what was projected?

Monitoring and Learning

- Was a marketing automation platform used?
- Were the messages sent out at the optimum times?
- Do we understand why some messages performed better than others?
- If the open-rate was strong, was the click-through rate similar?

- How does the latest campaign stack up against past campaigns?
- If the open and click-through rates were high, was the offer taken?

Testing and Adapting

- If the Subject appears to be the cause of a low open-rate, what is the proposed solution?
- Was A/B testing employed to learn which email performed best?
- What changes can be made to the content to get it to perform better?
- If the messaging seems strong, can the call-to-action or offer be altered to boost performance?
- Do the messages to the various audience segments need to be improved?
- Did the offer have *real* value?
- Did recipients recognize the sender?
- Was the call-to-action clear?
- Was the email seen as SPAM?

Writing with a Purpose

- Was the purpose immediately obvious?

- Was the message written with some personality?
- Did the message include a strong value component?
- Did the message focus on the donor and not on the organization?
- Was the message written in brief, active voice sentences?
- Was the NPO lingo (non-profit organization) removed?

> "**Remember, you're writing to a friend**—not someone on a call sheet."

Personalizing Your Message

- Did the message sound like it was coming from a friend?
- Did the email end with a personal touch?

> "***Pay No Attention to the Man Behind the Curtain***"

- Were personal aspects shared?
- Was common ground between the writer and reader sought?

Staying Donor-focused

> **Did you know?**
> The average donor retention rates for first-year offline-only donors is **29%**. The average donor retention rates for first-time online-only donors is **21%**.
> (Blackbaud's Charitable Giving Report)

- Did the message share the donor's passion?
- Are donors aware of how the funds are being spent?
- Are donors being made aware of the lives that are being changed?
- Are donors made to feel a part of the team?
- Does the donor feel communication is a two-way street?

Empowering with Trigger Words

- Were trigger words used?
- Did they cause action?

Delivering Value

- Is the reader's time being valued?
- Are you talking about what interests the reader most?
- Can the reader relate well to what's written?

Skipping the Non-profit Lingo

- Are you using "insider" language?
- Are you using acronyms that the reader understands?

Calling Readers to Act

- Are the calls-to-action clear, concise, and obvious?
- Are you using a mixture of textual and image calls-to-action?
- Is the call-to-action benefit-oriented?
- Does the call-to-action evoke curiosity?
- Does the call-to-action propose a solution?
- Are you using multiple calls-to-action?

Let's clarify here. We're not advocating multiple calls-to-action for several different offers. But, there's nothing wrong with having more than one call-to-cation for the same offer at the beginning and end of an email or in the middle and then again at the end of the message.

Choosing an Email Platform

- Was an email automation marketing system used?

- Does the email platform integrate well with the other moving parts of the organization?
- Are the reporting and analytics sufficient?
- Can you easily personalize the emails?

Uploading Your Contacts

- Were the email lists cleaned before starting?
- Was permission sought to add an individual's address to an email list?
- Were the different audiences segmented into separate lists?
- Have you considered the implications of complying with GDPR?

Creating Your First Campaign

- Does each team member understand their role and responsibilities?
- Was an email schedule developed?
- Have the metrics been decided upon?
- Will a landing page be employed to capture personal information?
- Will A/B testing be used to fine-tune the email campaign?
- Is the value proposition evident?

Making Sense of the Reports

- Were too few emails sent out to gauge success?
- Click-throughs mean more than opens. Conversions mean more than click-throughs.
- If the open-rate is lower than the national average, does the organization understand why?
- Is the unsubscribe rate high?
- Are the reports starting to show trends?

Chapter 23...

Sending Video Messages
(2 MIN READ)

L et's look at a technology that's making serious inroads into the way organizations send their messages – I'm talking about video email.

I started a live chat with a local video email provider, BombBomb.com, and asked one of their reps to send me a sample video email to start our conversation. Leo at BombBomb.com was quite helpful.

BombBomb.com lets you have a face-to-face conversation with those that matter most. BombBomb.com offers a 14-day free trial. We all know the more face-time we have the more conversions happen.

Here's what the email looks like when it lands in an in-box:

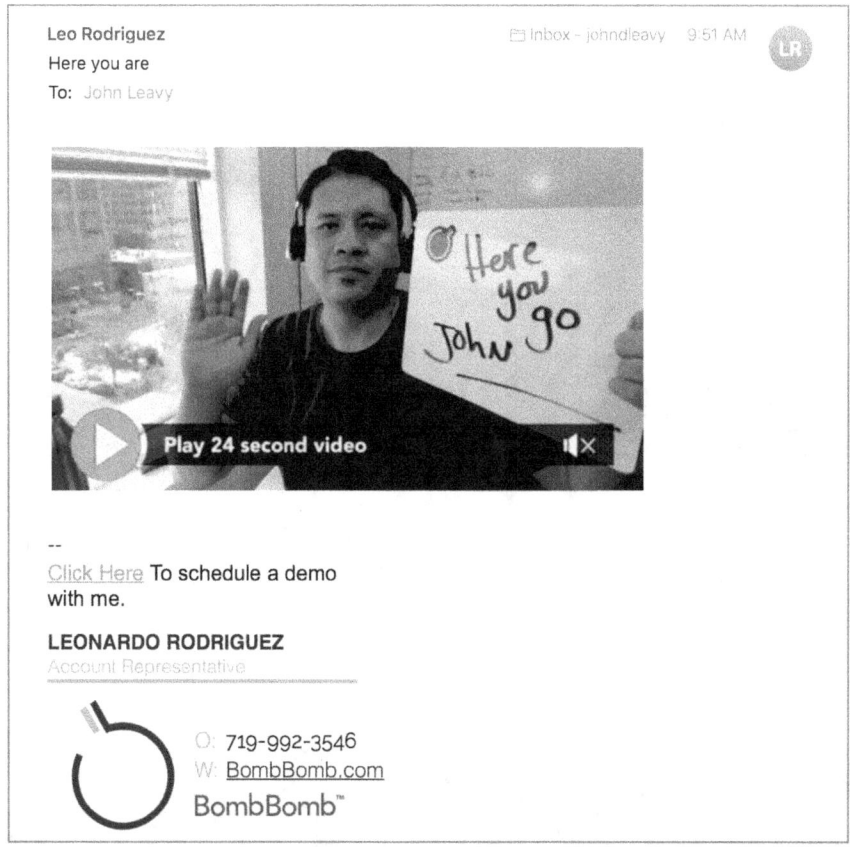

BombBomb.com allows you to quickly record, send, and track your video emails. Their platform provides: video email, social sharing, screen recording, video texting, and tracking analytics.

They offer a full sales platform with: automations, mass emails, lead capture forms, and done-for-you content.

Here are a few stats on the company's success:

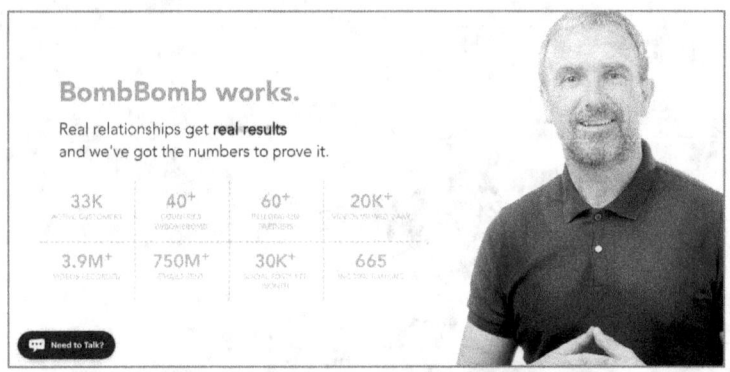

Check them out.

PART V

"The Payoff"

Chapter 24...

Announcing an Event by Email
(11 MIN READ)

Announcing an event by email will likely have the goals of **boosting the awareness** of the organization's cause and **building stronger relationships**. If the recipients that receive the messages forward those emails to their friends, then the goal of **collecting new names** would also be achieved.

It's not likely the primary objective of the email campaign itself would be to raise funds directly. (We'll talk about making an appeal by email in Chapter 26.) Let's suppose the event being announced is the annual fundraising dinner and some of the people find they cannot attend the event and instead opt to **send in an early**

donation. In that case, all four of the goals mentioned here would be achieved with one email campaign.

We need to examine two strategies when dissecting an event by email: the email being sent out and the strategy behind the campaign.

We'll cover the contents of the email message first, then talk about the campaign strategy.

Content of the Email

Let's take what we learned in Part III: *Writing Action-driven Content* and apply it to our email message that will be sent out announcing our event.

Ignite Your Email Campaign

The event in this example is that of a book launch.

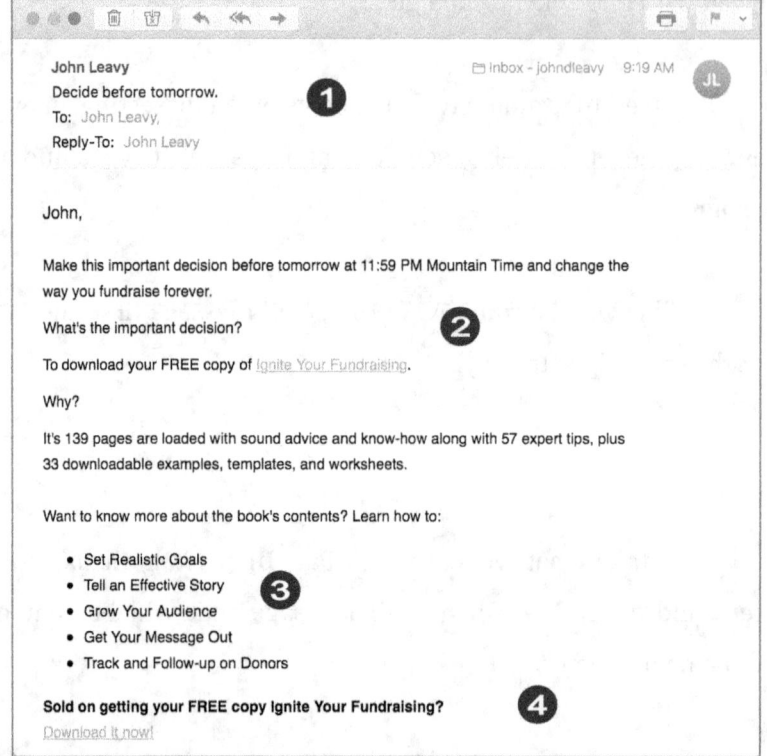

1. The email is sent from a real person with a Subject line that piques the recipient's interest. The salutation is also personalized.

2. The opening few sentences tell the purpose of the email and encourage the reader to take immediate action in downloading the free eBook.

3. The next couple of sentences give a description of the book's contents.

4. Another call to action is made.

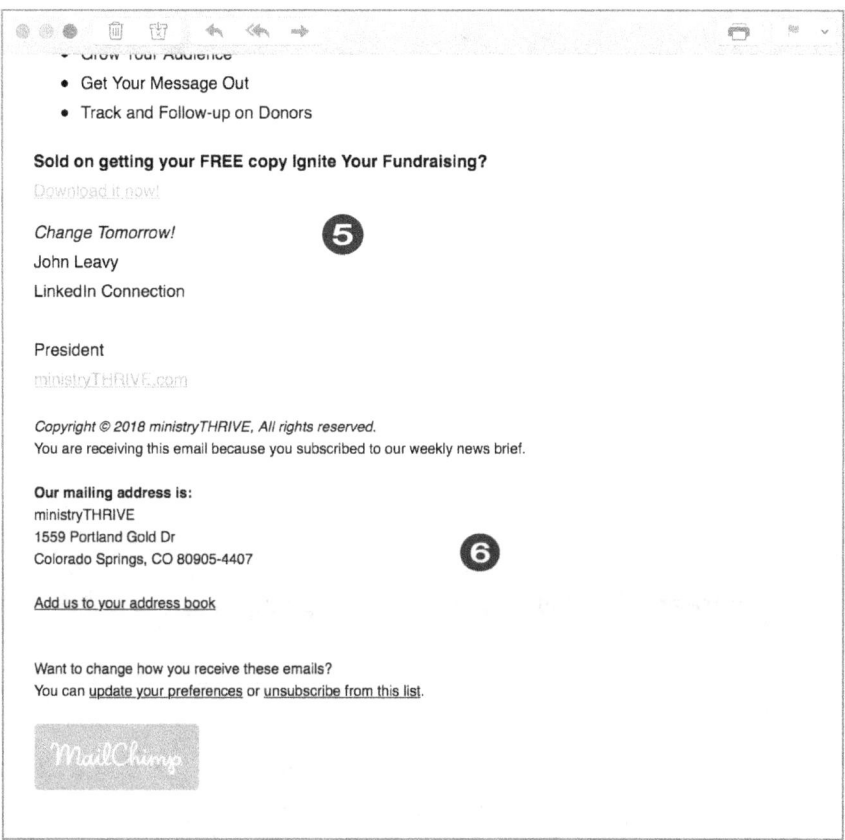

5. The closing is personal.

6. The organization's contact information is listed along with an unsubscribe link.

Strategy of the Campaign

As to the strategy of sending out emails through MailChimp, the names came from three sources: THRIVE5 the weekly news brief, a sampling of the 3,400 connections on LinkedIn, and names in the general contact file.

The email messages all went out on a Thursday morning or a Friday afternoon.

The THRIVE5 subscribers showed the best results (expected) followed by the LinkedIn connections, and then the general contacts.

Here are the results from THRIVE5 email:

0 Orders	$0.00 Average order revenue	$0.00 Total revenue
Open rate	40.5%	Click rate	4.8%
List average	35.0%	List average	4.0%
Industry average (Non-Profit)	19.5%	Industry average (Non-Profit)	1.9%
17 Opened	2 Clicked	0 Bounced	0 Unsubscribed

Ignite Your Email Campaign

Here are the results from the LinkedIn email:

Open rate	41.0%	Click rate	2.1%
List average	32.8%	List average	1.8%
Industry average (Non-Profit)	19.5%	Industry average (Non-Profit)	1.9%
197 Opened	10 Clicked	3 Bounced	29 Unsubscribed

The Unsubscribes might seem high but more than half of the LinkedIn connections are running commercial businesses and are not interested in non-profit fundraising.

Event Email Example (pg. 1)

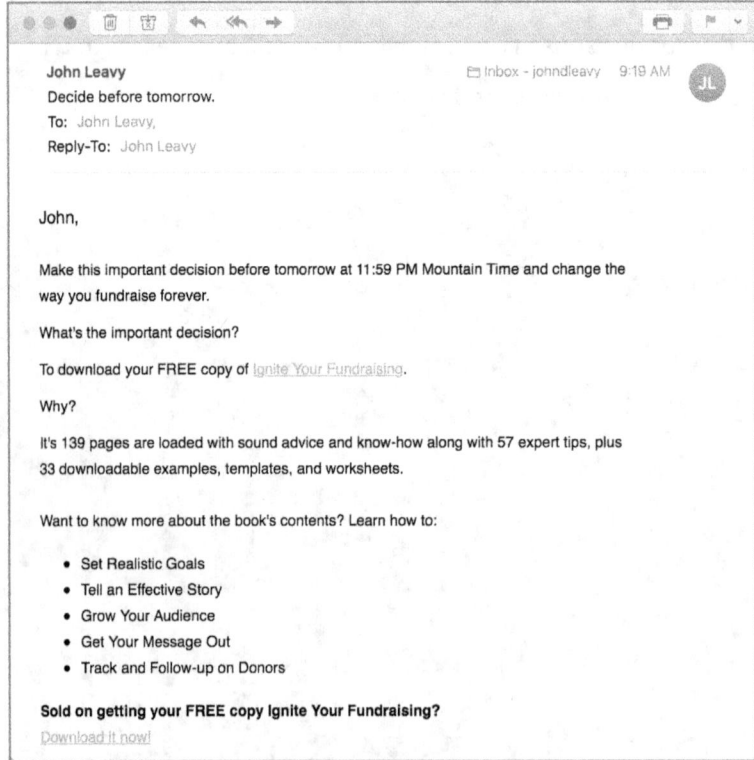

Download at:
ministryTHRIVE.com/IYE/DecideBeforeTomorrow.pdf

Event Email Example (pg. 2)

> - Grow Your Audience
> - Get Your Message Out
> - Track and Follow-up on Donors
>
> **Sold on getting your FREE copy Ignite Your Fundraising?**
> Download it now!
>
> *Change Tomorrow!*
> John Leavy
> LinkedIn Connection
>
> President
> ministryTHRIVE.com
>
> Copyright © 2018 ministryTHRIVE, All rights reserved.
> You are receiving this email because you subscribed to our weekly news brief.
>
> **Our mailing address is:**
> ministryTHRIVE
> 1559 Portland Gold Dr
> Colorado Springs, CO 80905-4407
>
> Add us to your address book
>
> Want to change how you receive these emails?
> You can update your preferences or unsubscribe from this list.
>
> *MailChimp*

Download at:
ministryTHRIVE.com/IYE/ DecideBeforeTomorrow.pdf

Chapter 25...

Doing a Giveaway by Email
(10 MIN READ)

Announcing a giveaway can apply to various freebees. The promotion might be a free eBook, a month-free membership, a tuition discount, tickets to the Big Game, or in the following example—an on-demand webinar that has already taken place.

Back in July 2018, I was asked by The Signatry, a Global Christian Foundation, to do a webinar on one of my latest books ***Ignite Your End-of-the-year Fundraising***.

I decided to give away a free digital copy of the book to entice people to register for the webinar.

The Signatry handled the email campaign announcing the webinar.

I gave the presentation.

 **Show & Tell:** Find a Giveaway Email Example at the end of this chapter.

Content of the Email

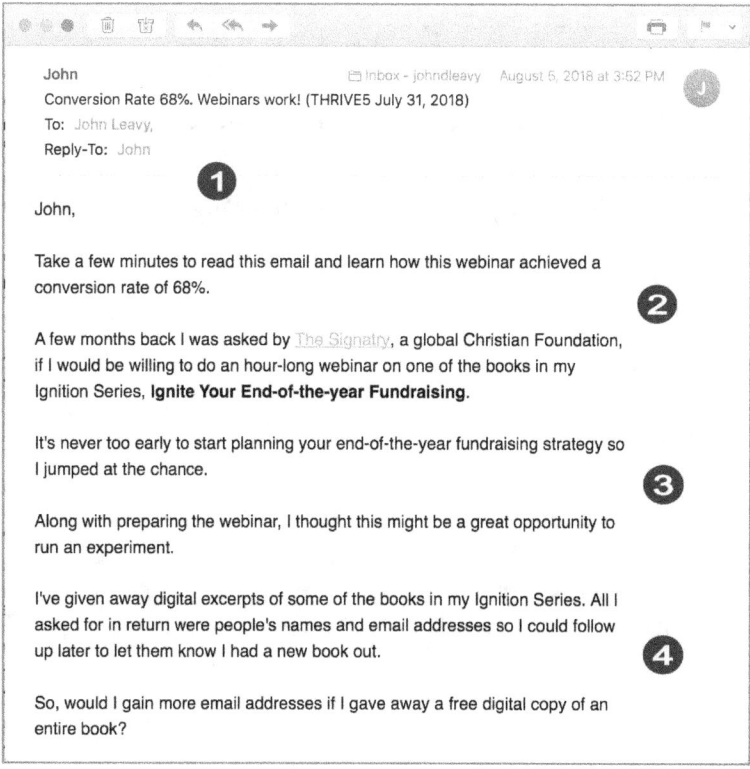

The email comes from a real person. The Subject sounds interesting. The communique is addressed to an individual. The email salutation is personalized.

1. The opening sentence gives the purpose of the message. The next sentence…A few months back…adds social proof to the book's contents. The Signatry, a Global Christian Foundation, believes **Ignite Your End-of-the-Year Fundraising** has value and wants it shared with its client base.

2. The next sentence plants the seed that it's never too early to think about EOY fundraising. The reader is then introduced to an experiment that will be run during the campaign.

3. The experiment is revealed—would more people take the opportunity to download the entire book instead of just an excerpt?

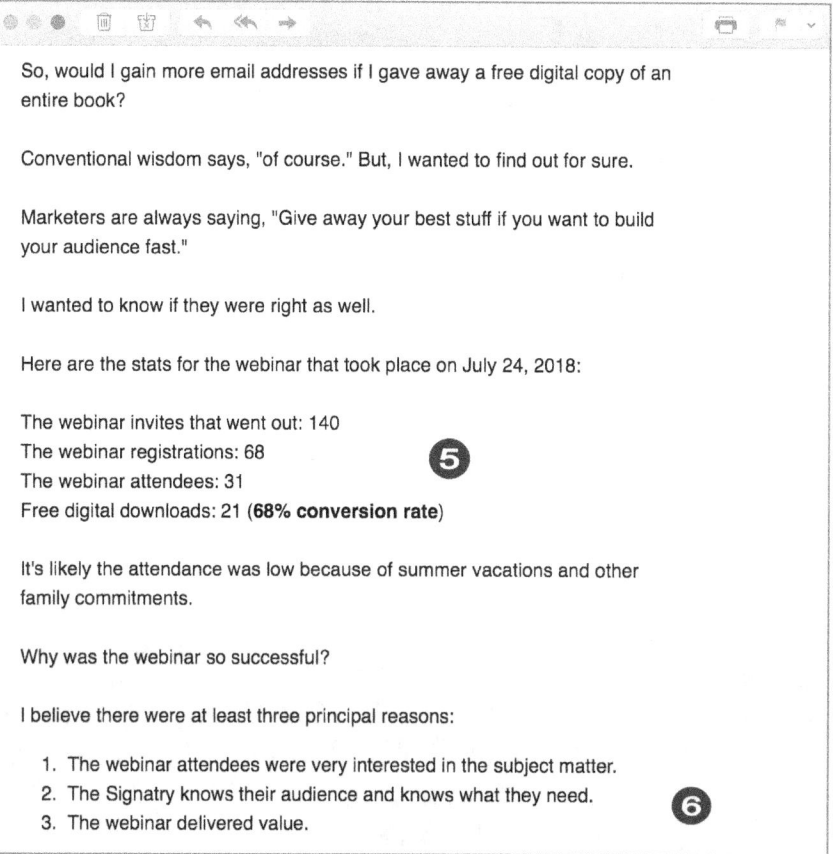

4. The statistics from the webinar are revealed.

5. The possible reasons the webinar was so successful are then outlined.

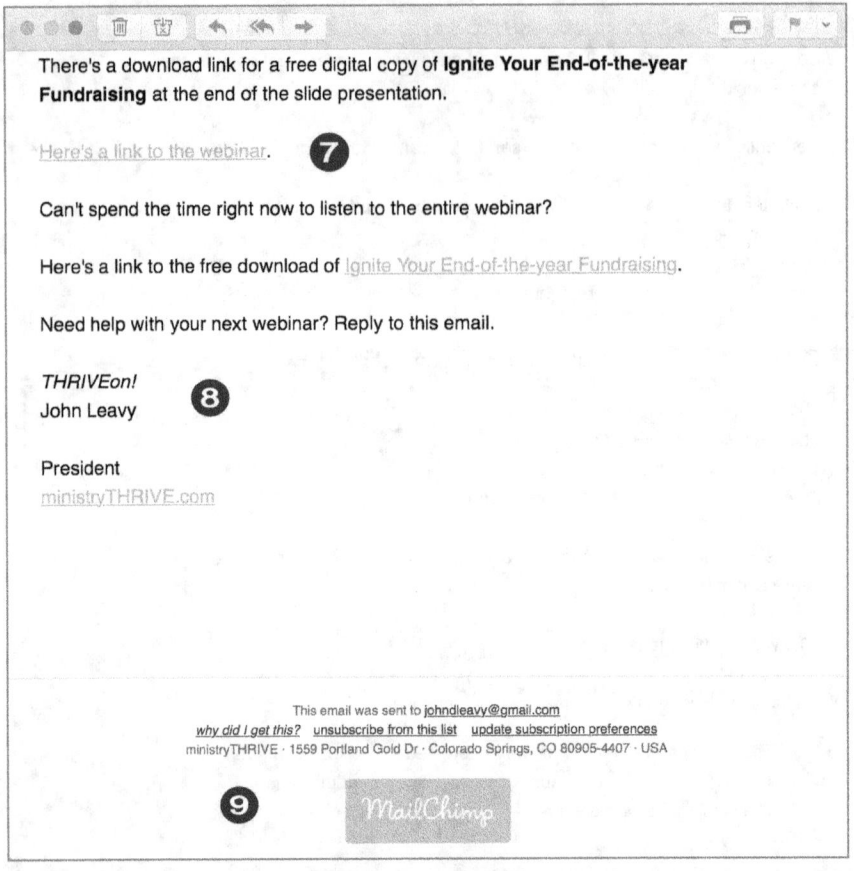

6. A link to watch the webinar followed by a link to the free digital download of *Ignite Your End-of-the-year Fundraising*.

7. The closing or valediction is also personalized.

8. The email was sent out using an email automation platform. The recipient has the option to unsubscribe from any further emails.

In our email example the recipients could either watch the webinar, download a free digital copy of the book, or do both.

Strategy of the Campaign

Let's breakdown the email so we can examine the strategy behind the communique:

The webinar was a rousing success. Here are the stats:

The webinar invites that went out: 140
The webinar registrations: 68
The webinar attendees: 31
Free digital downloads: 21 (**68% conversion rate**)

The average conversion rate for non-profits is 1.9%. Looks like the 68% conversion rate blew that statistic out of the water.

The attendance might seem low, but it was summer time after all and people surely had other plans on their minds.

There were probably three main reasons the webinar was successful.

1. The webinar attendees were very interested in the subject matter.

2. The Signatry obviously knows their audience well and what they need.
3. The webinar delivered value.

The Signatry's goal for holding the webinar was to get their non-profits to start thinking about their end-of-the-year fundraising plans in July not December.

I had three goals for the doing the webinar as well: reach an audience that likely has never heard of ministryTHRIVE, to boost people's awareness of what ministryTHRIVE is up to, and to acquire subscribers (new names, the webinar attendees that downloaded the free digital copy of ***Ignite Your End-of-the-year Fundraising***.)

It's not going to be difficult to measure the overall success of the giveaway strategy. Either the email recipients saw value in what was being offered for free, and took it, or they did not.

Let's look at what could foil a giveaway strategy.

- Perhaps the timing (day and time) of the email campaign was not the best
- Perchance the Subject of the email was not enticing enough
- Suppose the email went out to an audience that would appreciate the gift

- What if the content of the message was not action-driven
- Maybe the giveaway was not explained well enough
- Perhaps the wrong item was chosen to be given away
- What if the giveaway process was too complicated
- Suppose too much personal information was requested
- Perchance the giveaway lacked luster
- What if the giveaway period was too short
- Perhaps the free gift was seen as having less value than the personal information requested

Adjust where necessary and give it a second go.

Ignite Your Email Campaign

Giveaway Email Example (pg. 1)

John   Inbox - johndleavy   August 5, 2018 at 3:52 PM

Conversion Rate 68%. Webinars work! (THRIVE5 July 31, 2018)

To: John Leavy,

Reply-To: John

John,

Take a few minutes to read this email and learn how this webinar achieved a conversion rate of 68%.

A few months back I was asked by The Signatry, a global Christian Foundation, if I would be willing to do an hour-long webinar on one of the books in my Ignition Series, **Ignite Your End-of-the-year Fundraising**.

It's never too early to start planning your end-of-the-year fundraising strategy so I jumped at the chance.

Along with preparing the webinar, I thought this might be a great opportunity to run an experiment.

I've given away digital excerpts of some of the books in my Ignition Series. All I asked for in return were people's names and email addresses so I could follow up later to let them know I had a new book out.

So, would I gain more email addresses if I gave away a free digital copy of an entire book?

Download at:
ministryTHRIVE.com/IYE/ConversionRate68%.pdf

Ignite Your Email Campaign

Giveaway Email Example (pg. 2)

So, would I gain more email addresses if I gave away a free digital copy of an entire book?

Conventional wisdom says, "of course." But, I wanted to find out for sure.

Marketers are always saying, "Give away your best stuff if you want to build your audience fast."

I wanted to know if they were right as well.

Here are the stats for the webinar that took place on July 24, 2018:

The webinar invites that went out: 140
The webinar registrations: 68
The webinar attendees: 31
Free digital downloads: 21 (**68% conversion rate**)

It's likely the attendance was low because of summer vacations and other family commitments.

Why was the webinar so successful?

I believe there were at least three principal reasons:

1. The webinar attendees were very interested in the subject matter.
2. The Signatry knows their audience and knows what they need.
3. The webinar delivered value.

Download at:
ministryTHRIVE.com/IYE/ConversionRate68%.pdf

181 *Chapter 25/Doing a Giveaway by Email*

Giveaway Email Example (pg. 3)

There's a download link for a free digital copy of **Ignite Your End-of-the-year Fundraising** at the end of the slide presentation.

Here's a link to the webinar.

Can't spend the time right now to listen to the entire webinar?

Here's a link to the free download of Ignite Your End-of-the-year Fundraising.

Need help with your next webinar? Reply to this email.

THRIVEon!
John Leavy

President
ministryTHRIVE.com

This email was sent to johndleavy@gmail.com
why did I get this?   unsubscribe from this list   update subscription preferences
ministryTHRIVE · 1559 Portland Gold Dr · Colorado Springs, CO 80905-4407 · USA

MailChimps

Download at:
ministryTHRIVE.com/IYE/ConversionRate68%.pdf

Chapter 26...

Making an Appeal by Email
(12 MIN READ)

A ppeal letters can have several objectives. The letter could be an appeal for an end-of-the-year gift, for monthly financial support, or to fund a special project.

Newsletters sent out monthly or email updates that have a link at the end of the message inferring the recipient should visit the organization's donation page, are not effective appeal methods.

In some instances, an appeal letter might go out soliciting volunteers, needed supplies, or resources. The appeal may not always be about raising funds.

Appeal letters have a definite, understood by both parties, purpose. The organization is looking for help or assistance of some sort.

 Appeal letters are all about the donor not the organization.

Appeal letters should differ from every other communique the person receives from the organization.

In the Appeal Letter Example that follows, constituents are asked to financially support Project:Caleb's speaking opportunity at the June 2019 Association of Gospel Rescue Missions Conference in Nashville, Tennessee. (Made up event for this illustration.)

The appeal was made within an email message and not sent in letter form.

Clearly, this appeal goes out to a select group of faithful donors, and not the organization's entire contact list.

Let's dissect the email message so we understand what the vital elements are.

Ignite Your Email Campaign

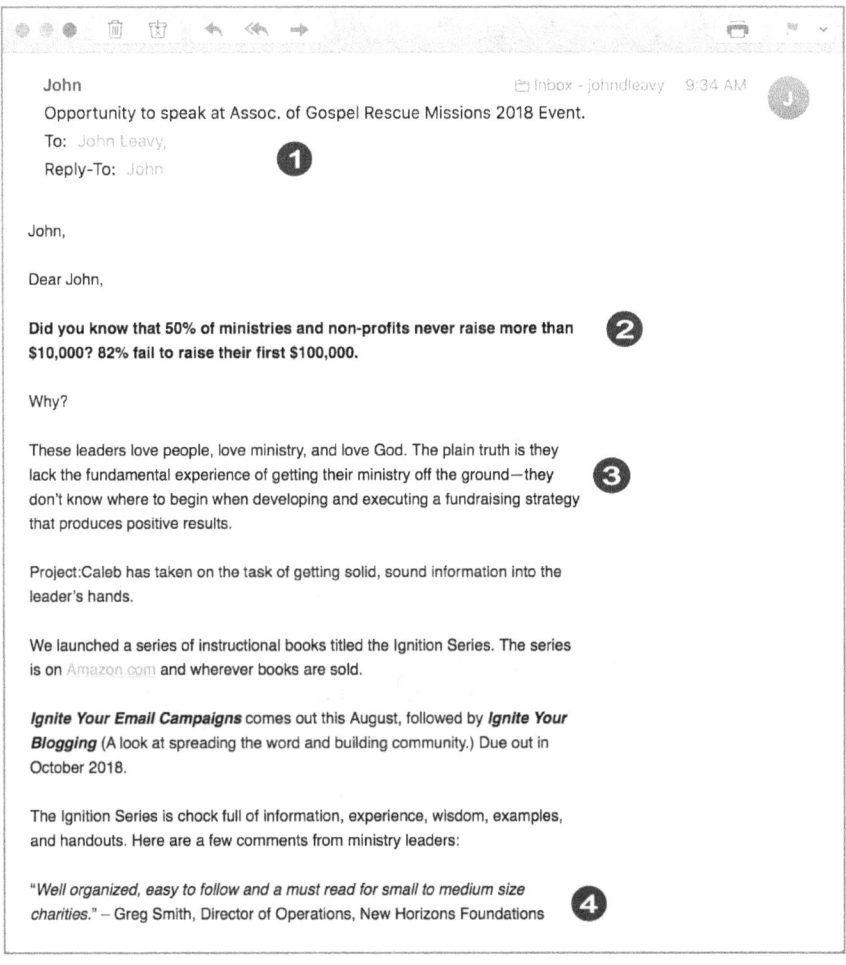

1. The email is sent from a real person. It is also personalized with the recipient's first name.

2. Think about including a statistic to add authority and legitimacy to the needed-support argument as a regular staple of our appeal letters. Here we added: ***Did you know***

that 50% of ministries and non-profits never raise more than $10,000? 82% fail to raise their first $100,000. Statistics let people know how urgent and massive the problem. The recipients also become aware the organization is on top of the situation—connected, they know what's happening.

3. The opening sentences should set the stage for the discussion. It should explain the problem and talk about the organization's solution.

4. It's always good to add an authoritative voice or two to back up the organization's approach in solving the problem. Here two testimonial quotes are added.

Ignite Your Email Campaign

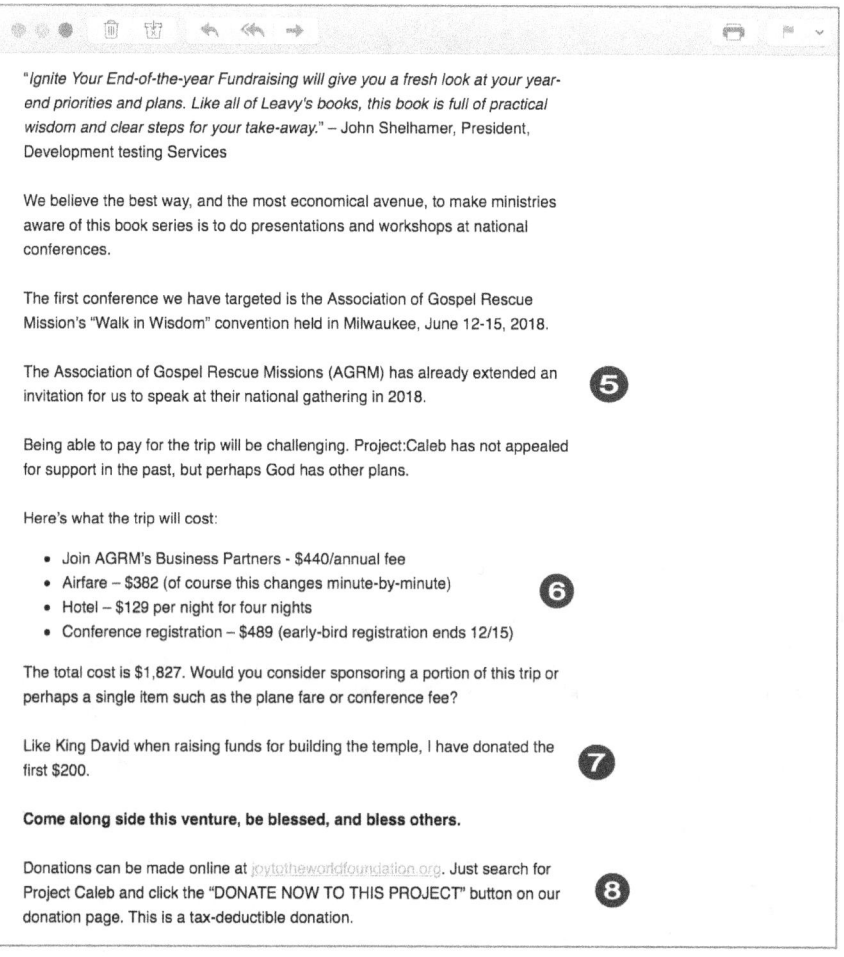

5. People need to know when things are happening. In this case, the first conference speaking opportunity takes place June 15 thru 18, 2018.

6. It's important to give donors the details on how much is needed and how the money will be spent. In this example,

the membership fee, airfare, hotel and conference fee are itemized.

7. It never hurts to refer to the most authoritative source on this planet. Here, King David's financial support for building God's temple is mentioned. Project:Caleb is also noting that its founder is donating the first $200. Are the leadership and advisory board members financially supporting the organization's efforts?

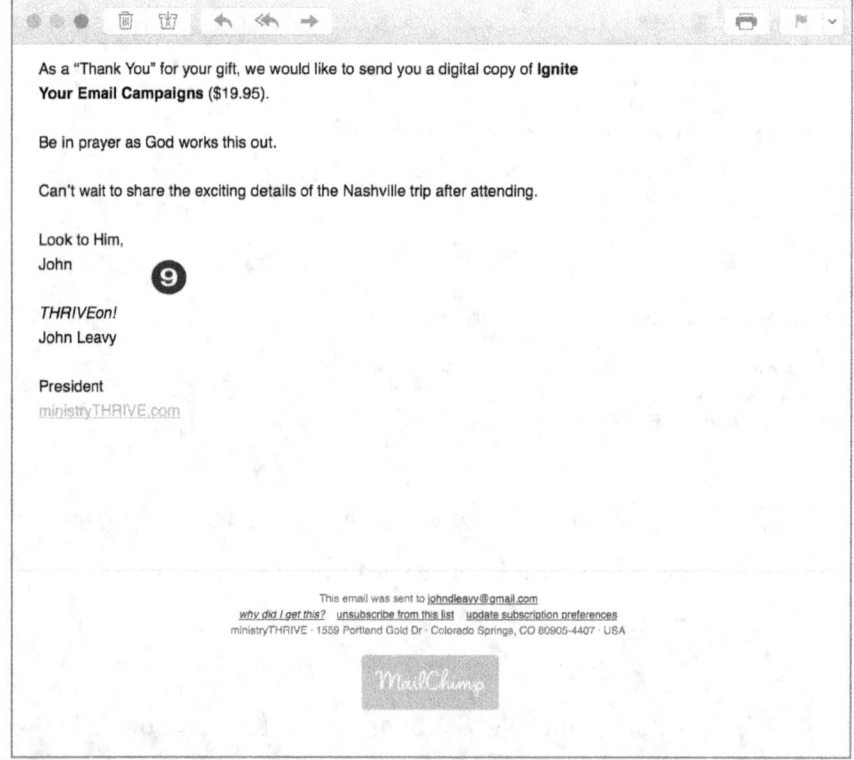

8. **How to Donate** – If the person receiving the appeal letter is to do something, they must be told to do so. The gifting process must be obvious, secure, and flawless.

9. **Closing** – The closing should thank the person in advance for their time and consideration. Make the close personal. Its appeal needs to come from a real person.

Measuring the Appeal Letter's Success

The appeal letter whether sent by email or the US Post Office, a strategy needs to be in place.

Let's look at some possible causes as to why the appeal letter performed poorly.

- Have the right potential supporters been identified?

- Does the letter take the reader through a logical progression of the problem and the organization's solution?

- Does the reader understand the purpose of the letter?

- Does the reader understand the urgency?

- Does the reader feel they can be a part of the solution?

- Does the appeal/solution make sense to the reader?

- Does the email message have a professional look-and-feel?

- Is there a good balance of whitespace, text, and images?

- Was an attention-grabbing headline used?

- Is the email too long?

- Does the information convey passion and excitement? Is it timely, relevant, interesting, and donor-centric?

- Is the need clearly explained and justified?

- Are the supportive details included?

- Is the content free from spelling, grammatical, and other typographical errors?

- Have any authoritative voices been added?

- Is there a mechanism for people to ask questions?

- Is the donation process secure, and trouble-free?

- Can the reader easily share the appeal letter with family and friends?

 Get in the habit of using the words "you" and "yours" more than "we" and "us." Words such as "you" immediately bring the reader into the story.

- Focus on impact. How are people's lives being changed? How is the problem getting better? What life's challenges existed before that do not exist now?

- How are the funds going to be used? It is important people know their money is being spent wisely.

 Find an Appeal Letter Example at the end of this chapter.

 Stick to one concern in the letter. Don't use it as a catch-all for everything the organization wants to do over the next few years.

 Show passion.

Use POWERFUL words.

- Was the donor given a deadline?

 **If the appeal letter is not producing positive results, change things. Try different openings, various stories, diverse calls-to-action.**

 Don't expect the results to get better unless you better things first.

Appeal Letter Example (pg. 1)

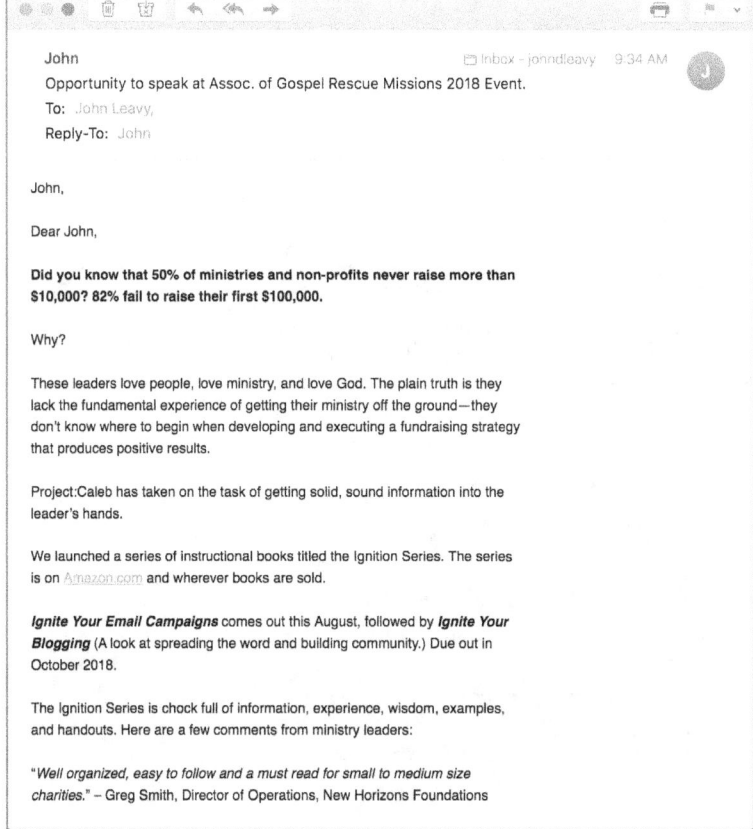

Download at:

ministryTHRIVE.com/IYE/OpportunityToSpeak.pdf

Appeal Letter Example (pg. 2)

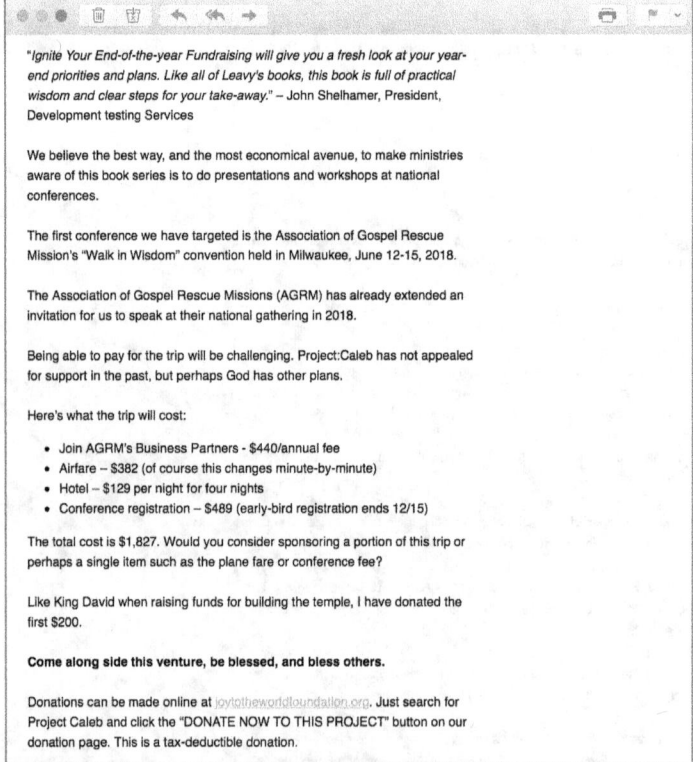

Download at:

ministryTHRIVE.com/IYE/OpportunityToSpeak.pdf

Ignite Your Email Campaign

Appeal Letter Example (pg. 3)

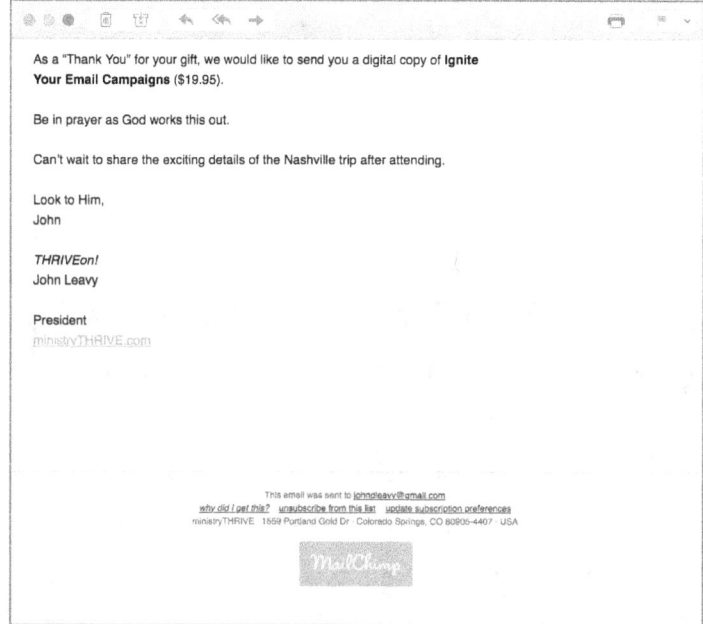

Download at:
ministryTHRIVE.com/IYE/OpportunityToSpeak.pdf

195 Chapter 26/Making an Appeal by Email

Chapter 27...

Delivering a Newsletter by Email

(17 MIN READ)

N ewsletters can be short or long. They can deal with one subject or have a broader focus. The writing can be in-depth or brief. The format might be in plain-text or designed using a slick template. The publication may be loaded with links to click-on plus scores of interesting images. The stories might range from informative, educational, or promotional. The publication might come out weekly, monthly, quarterly, or at some other schedule time.

> "Before jumping into publishing a newsletter, ask yourself—**Is a newsletter for me; do I like to write?**"

In this chapter we'll talk about two different newsletter formats that can be delivered by email. The first publication example is constructed in an at-a-glance format. The email is brief. Full of short sentences with hyperlinks to more information. The reader can quickly scan the message and decide what story interests them most.

The second newsletter format is more conversational, more personal. Only one subject is tackled.

The campaign method to deliver the newsletters is the same.

Contents of the (brief) Email

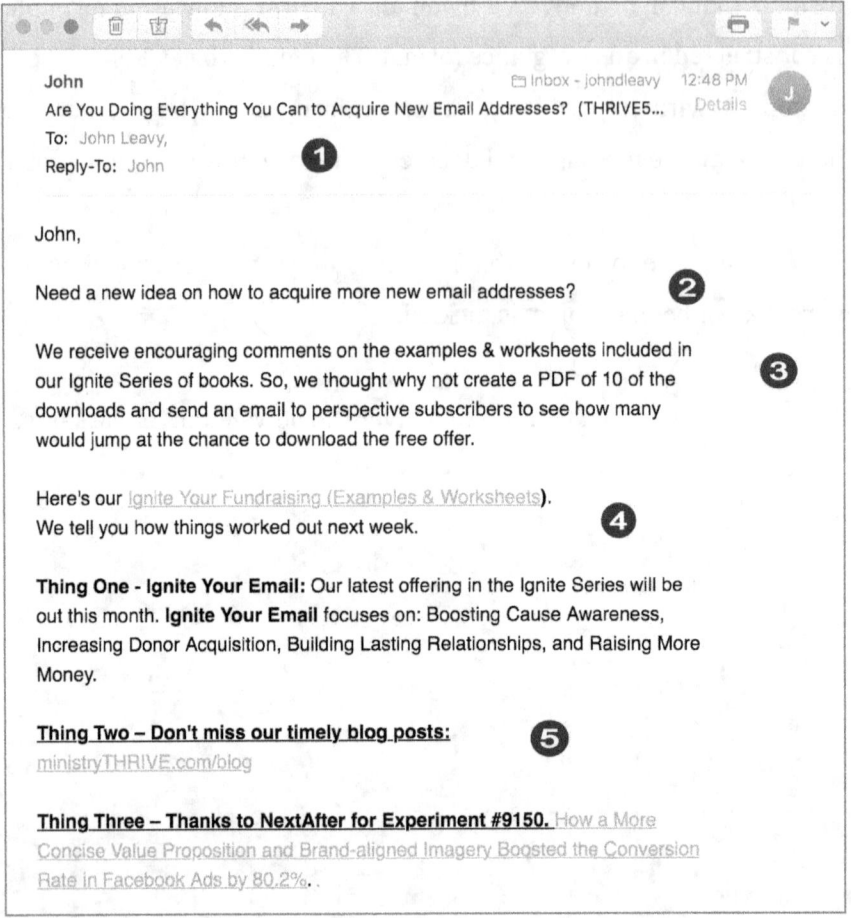

1. The email is sent from a real person. The Subject asks a question many non-profits struggle with all year.
2. The opening sentence makes a promise.
3. Social proof is added.
4. A download link is provided towards the beginning.

5. The weekly news brief, THRIVE5, highlights five subjects that are likely on the reader's mind.

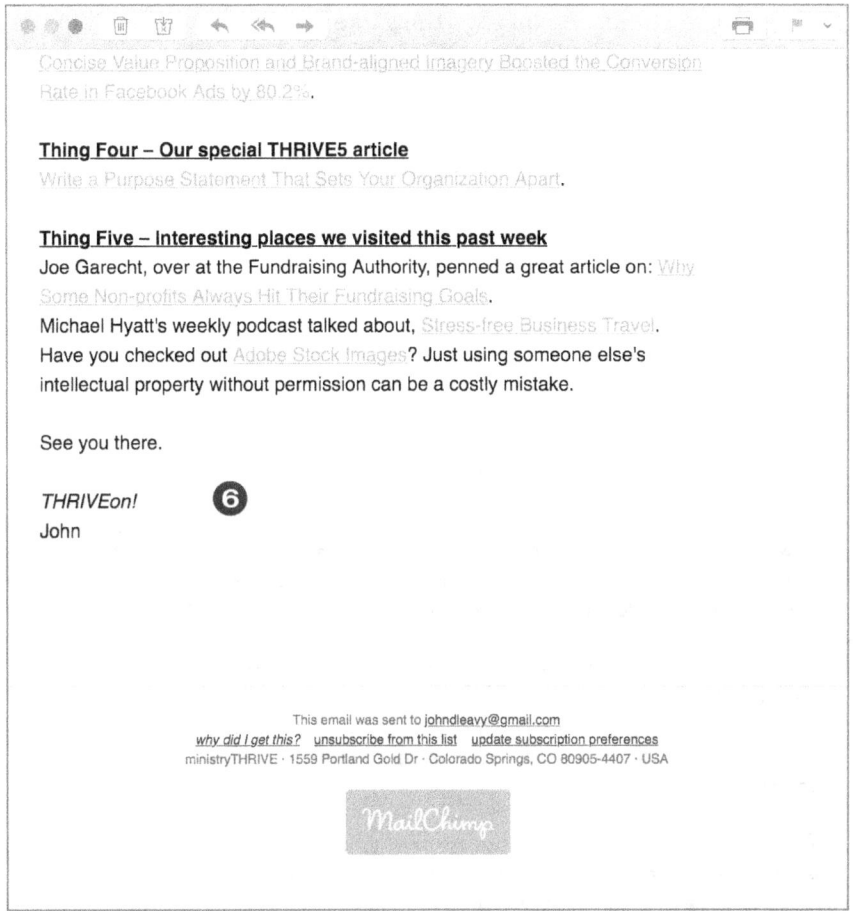

6. The email has a personal closing and gives the reader the options to opt out of any further communiques.

Contents of the (single-subject) Email

The single-subject email uses the same message mentioned in the Giveaway Email example. Refer back to Chapter 25 for a breakdown of this email.

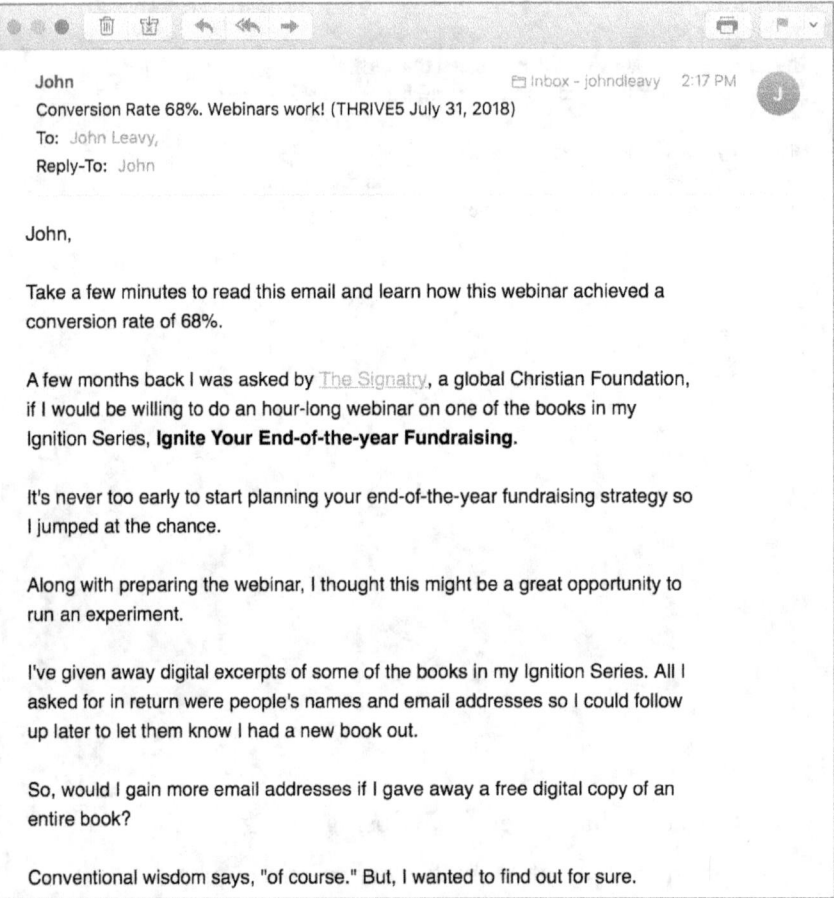

Strategy of the Campaign

The newsletter strategy is different from a regular email campaign in that it will be ongoing, never ending. Let's look at the elements that go into delivering a newsletter on some consistent basis.

Mission would be the first element to tackle. Why invest the necessary time, resources, and talent? Newsletters are resource hogs, time bandits. What if it were decided the mission of the newsletter was two-fold: first, to inform, educate and engage and second, to begin to build relationships that lead the readership to become involved in the work of the organization.

Purpose is the next ingredient to explore. The *mission* is what we do, and the *purpose* is why we do it. Wired Impact is an organization that builds websites for non-profits. They believe the Internet is a tool that is to be used for good. They further surmise better relationships happen. Their job focuses on empowering non-profits they work with and they think tangible results should drive everything they do.

Knowing the Audience is the cornerstone to any publication's success. What does the reader think is relevant, important? What problems do they believe need solving? What are they passionate about seeing happen? How do they measure impact, success? It's vital the writer knows what the reader wants to see happen.

> "*I have made this longer than usual because I have not had the time to make it shorter.*"—Blaise Pascal

Attention-grabbing Headlines ensure the publication is read. Craft, craft, and recraft the story headlines to make sure they immediately grab the reader's attention. It takes more time and attention to make headlines succinic. The stories, no matter how interesting or noteworthy, won't be read if the headlines never draw the reader into the story.

> **Did you know?**
> Organizations choose email **66%** of the time as their preferred method to send newsletters.

Newsworthy means what's being shared is: interesting, notable, important, significant, momentous, historic, remarkable, sensational, unprecedented, groundbreaking. Newsworthy does not mean one person knows something another individual does not.

Offer Value to the readership to keep them coming back. Does the publication answer a question, build relationships, serve an audience, address a need, solve a problem, encourage participation or action, inspire engagement, rally the troops? The reader is spending the time reading the publication. What are they receiving in return?

The **Format** of the newsletter needs to serve the needs of the writer as well as its readership. The publication may be short or long. It may have one story or several features. Will it be branded? What fonts and images should be used? Should links be used to send readers to more information, the organization's website, or social page?

The **Layout** of the publication is important as well. Should the newsletter use a template or be done in plain-text? Should it be done in a magazine or newspaper style? Will all the headlines be at the top of the publication with links to the balance of the stories for quick access? Should readers be sent to the organization's blog to read the rest of the accounts?

Correct Timing can build or break a publication. Will the newsletter go to press weekly, monthly, or quarterly? Know your limitations. Start out slow and then increase your efforts as interest and circulation build. Monthly may be the perfect timeframe.

Consistency raises people's expectations and creates anticipation and interest. Set a publication schedule and stick to it.

Everyone's time and attention are being strained today. If readers know the newsletter comes out on the first Tuesday of each month, they'll start anticipating its arrival.

The **Professional Look-and-feel** of a newsletter reflects directly on the organization. There are literally hundreds of free options to acquire professionally designed email templates—some simple, some quite complex. Many of them even offer plain-text options so you can skip the strict formatting but still track the metrics and give people the option to unsubscribe.

Show some **Personality** when writing. Let the reader get to know you. Who you are. What you believe. What's important to you. Write conversationally. Let people in on why it's so important to do the work you're doing.

> **Did you know?**
> When asked which medium people would like to receive updates from, **90%** preferred an email newsletter.

Stay **Reader-centric**. It's imperative the reader know what's being accomplished is because of their involvement and support. Focus more on using *second person* plural pronouns such as "you" and "yours" than *first person* plurals like "us," and "we." Writing in *first person* removes the reader from the story.

Calls-to Action must be clear, concise, and obvious. Don't assume the reader will finish the newsletter and immediately draw the conclusion on what he or she needs to do next. It won't happen. If you want the reader's opinion, ask them to take a survey. If you want them to sign-up for something, ask them. If you want them to click on a link, make the request. People need to be shown, steered, guided.

Make it **Mobile Friendly**. If the newsletter is not mobile-friendly, it may not be read by the entire audience. **54%** of smartphone owners use their devices to check their email. By the end of 2018 the number is expected to be **80%**. **70%** of recipients delete emails immediately that don't render, display well on mobile devices. Go mobile or go home.

Always Source Your Material. It's important to credit any source used in the publication. It adds credibility and authenticity. It also avoids costly court trials and poor publicity.

Getting the newsletter into the reader's hands can take several tracks, we've opted here to do it by email:

- The publication might reside on the website. An email is sent out with a link back to the document. This method creates more website traffic and gives people the opportunity to look around the site.

- The publication might be attached to an email or the newsletter may comprise the bulk of email copy itself.

- The newsletter could be printed out, passed out, or mailed to donors who do not have access to the Internet.

 Find two Newsletter Examples at the end of this chapter.

> **Did you know?**
> Focusing on what people receive verses what they have to do boosts the conversion rate by **44%**.
> (NextAfter.com Experiment #1621)

Use whatever method works best for you and your supporters.

 Don't tell people to sign up, tell them what they'll receive when they do.

Measuring the Newsletter's Success

Once strategies are in place for the newsletter, the success rate needs to be measured. If the goal of the newsletter is to inform and educate potential supporters and donors, it's going to be difficult to determine if people are reading the publication unless they take some action. Action in the form of sending an email your way, visiting the website, joining in on social media discussions or making a gift from the donation page.

If the goal of the publication is to turn potential supporters into donors, then the only measurement we'll have is if they make a gift to the cause.

If you're trying to get the readership to act by leaving their email address, then subscriptions will be the determining factor.

If the newsletter is enclosed in an email and sent by way of a vehicle such as MailChimp or ConstantContact we'll be able to tell if people received the publication and opened the message, but not whether they read what was sent. Readers will need to take some action to confirm that fact.

 Google Analytics can be leveraged to track if readers visit the website or social channels.

It's good that people are reading the newsletter and becoming informed on what the organization is accomplishing. But if the goal is to get people to engage or give, then they must take some action.

Several statistics in this chapter courtesy of: Statistics that Prove Email Marketing is (Still) Not Dead, posted by Caroline Malamut on February 4, 2016.

Ignite Your Email Campaign

Email Newsletter Example 1 (pg. 1)

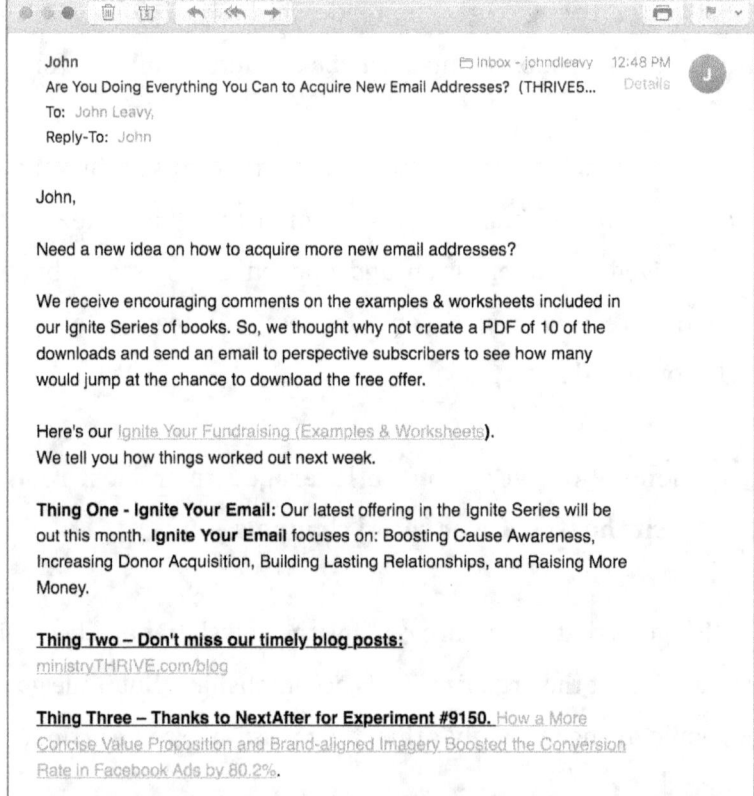

Ignite Your Email Campaign

Email Newsletter
Example 1 (pg. 2)

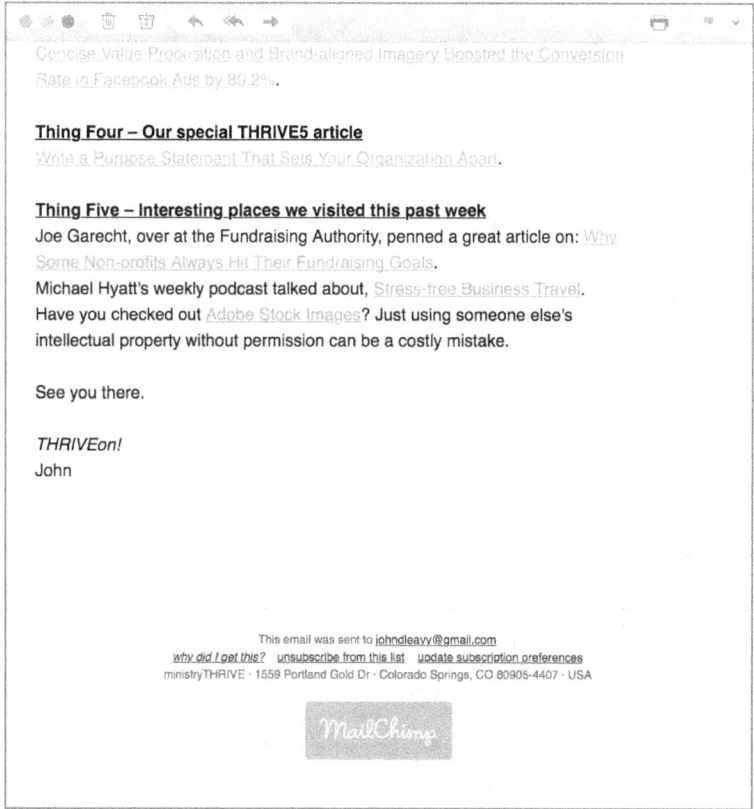

Download at:

ministryTHRIVE.com/IYE/AreYouDoingEverything.pdf

Ignite Your Email Campaign

Email Newsletter Example 2 (pg. 1)

John Inbox - johndleavy 2:17 PM

Conversion Rate 68%. Webinars work! (THRIVE5 July 31, 2018)

To: John Leavy,

Reply-To: John

John,

Take a few minutes to read this email and learn how this webinar achieved a conversion rate of 68%.

A few months back I was asked by The Signatry, a global Christian Foundation, if I would be willing to do an hour-long webinar on one of the books in my Ignition Series, **Ignite Your End-of-the-year Fundraising**.

It's never too early to start planning your end-of-the-year fundraising strategy so I jumped at the chance.

Along with preparing the webinar, I thought this might be a great opportunity to run an experiment.

I've given away digital excerpts of some of the books in my Ignition Series. All I asked for in return were people's names and email addresses so I could follow up later to let them know I had a new book out.

So, would I gain more email addresses if I gave away a free digital copy of an entire book?

Conventional wisdom says, "of course." But, I wanted to find out for sure.

Download at:

ministryTHRIVE.com/IYE/ConversionRate68.pdf

Email Newsletter Example 2 (pg. 2)

Marketers are always saying, "Give away your best stuff if you want to build your audience fast."

I wanted to know if they were right as well.

Here are the stats for the webinar that took place on July 24, 2018:

The webinar invites that went out: 140
The webinar registrations: 68
The webinar attendees: 31
Free digital downloads: 21 (**68% conversion rate**)

It's likely the attendance was low because of summer vacations and other family commitments.

Why was the webinar so successful?

I believe there were at least three principal reasons:

1. The webinar attendees were very interested in the subject matter.
2. The Signatry knows their audience and knows what they need.
3. The webinar delivered value.

There's a download link for a free digital copy of **Ignite Your End-of-the-year Fundraising** at the end of the slide presentation.

Here's a link to the webinar.

Can't spend the time right now to listen to the entire webinar?

Download at:

ministryTHRIVE.com/IYE/ConversionRate68.pdf

Ignite Your Email Campaign

Email Newsletter
Example 2 (pg. 3)

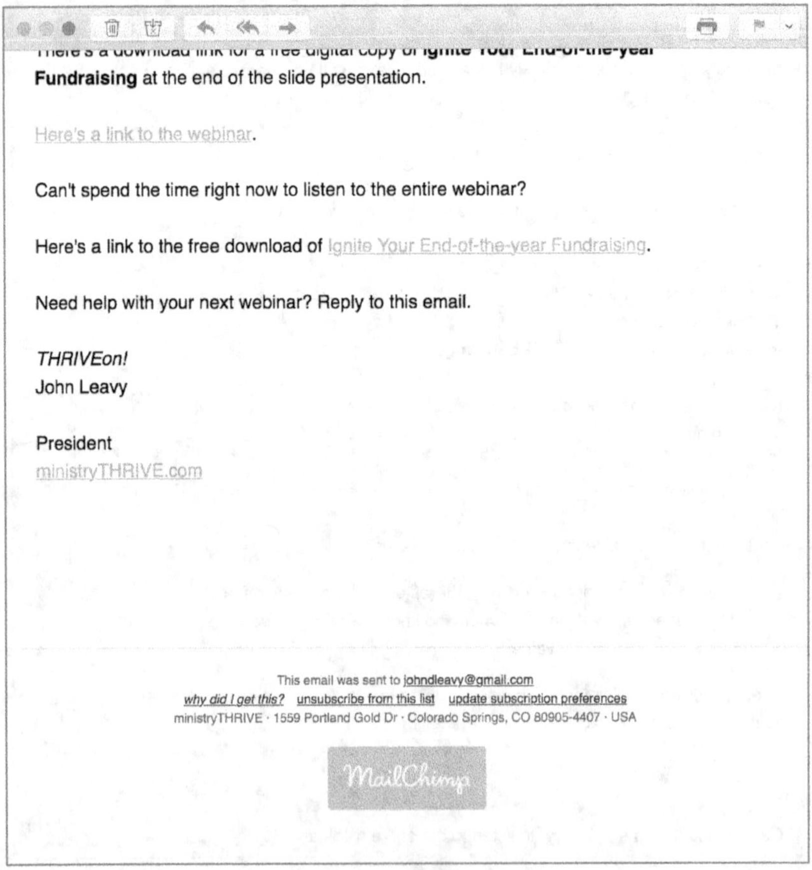

There's a download link for a free digital copy of **Ignite Your End-of-the-year Fundraising** at the end of the slide presentation.

Here's a link to the webinar.

Can't spend the time right now to listen to the entire webinar?

Here's a link to the free download of Ignite Your End-of-the-year Fundraising.

Need help with your next webinar? Reply to this email.

THRIVEon!
John Leavy

President
ministryTHRIVE.com

This email was sent to johndleavy@gmail.com
why did I get this?   unsubscribe from this list   update subscription preferences
ministryTHRIVE · 1559 Portland Gold Dr · Colorado Springs, CO 80905-4407 · USA

MailChimp

Download at:

ministryTHRIVE.com/IYE/AreYouDoingEverything.pdf

Chapter 28...

Sharing a Blog Post by Email
(8 MIN READ)

It's unreasonable to expect your blog readership to head over to your blog on a regular basis to see what brilliance you've recently penned. People are busy. If you decide to blog weekly, why not post your article on your blog and send people an email towards the end of the week telling them what they're missing.

> **Did you know?**
> Bloggers that post daily get **5X** more traffic.

Or, if you post three to five times per week, why not send out a quick email at week's end with opening sentences from each article and links back to the posts. That way the recipients could quickly scan the email, and decide which article interests them most and read that one.

> **Did you know?**
> Blog posts with images get **94%** more views.

Contents of the Email

Don't abuse your readership's good nature by sending them blog posts that resemble novelettes or short stories. That's not what people's in-boxes are for. Those posts will not be read no matter how interesting the subject.

People visit blogs when they believe they have the time to soak up a little more information or words of wisdom. The post used in this example is around 550 words.

Some people post longer articles and others shorter. You'll have to get to know your readership to see what works best for them, not you.

The website only provides a one-way communication channel. The blog allows for a second lane of interaction that draws the reader into the conversation. People can read the blog postings and make their comments. They can also read what others have written.

Consider what makes a blog amazing, and then think about how the blog might be used strategically in your organization.

Megan Totka over at Forbes.com wrote an article titled, The 8 Essential Elements of a Successful Post. Here's what Megan had to say:

1. Magnetic headline
2. Compelling lead sentence
3. Useful subheads
4. Informative and engaging body
5. Appealing graphics
6. Powerful call-to-action
7. Relevant internal link
8. Good meta description

I would add, the useful subhead should continue to pique the reader's interest and support the story being told. The appealing graphics go beyond good-looking images of beautiful places. The images, sometimes referred to as hero images should be esthetically pleasing to the eye, they should convey emotion, passion, progress being made, lives being changed—positive results being accrued. The internal links should give the reader a chance to dig deeper and learn more.

For those unfamiliar with the term, meta description, it is the snippet Google displays in the search results.

Strategy of the Campaign

An organization might have several objectives in emailing blog posts to their readership. They may want to keep people informed who have not had the time to read the blog.

They may see the email campaign as a way of strengthening the relationship.

They could also see the email campaign as a way of generating traffic to their website. People click on the link in the email, stop by the site to read the blog post and then decide to look around the balance of the website.

Sending people your blog posts by email may be your, "Hold the Puppy", strategy. Thinking if they like your blog articles they'll love your new book.

The blog posts could be used as an opportunity to tell your readership about the new product, service or project you've just started.

Blog posts can be a great way of reintroducing the organization to people.

Perhaps you could use the post to tell your readers you just opened an outpost on Twitter, Facebook, or Instagram.

Emailing people your blog posts is a great way to stay in touch. People get busy. They get bombarded with information. Emailing people with your posts on a regular basis is the perfect prescription for staying in their consciousness.

Emailing people your posts could someday turn potential supporters into donors.

Blog Post Email Example (pg. 1)

John Leavy Inbox - johndleavy 1:36 PM
Write a Purpose Statement That Sets Your Organization Apart
To: John Leavy,
Reply-To: John Leavy

John,

Over the years, people have confused and misused these three assertions: Purpose, Mission and Vision.

Some get confused on which to apply when talking or writing.

But let's not concern ourselves with other people's misuse of these statements. Let's make sure we have a good understanding of what each means and be able to explain and use them with our donors, supporters and the people we meet.

Here's an easy way to remember which term means what:

The Statement of Purpose – is why the organization exists and why it has decided to make a difference.
The Mission Statement – is the path the organization sets to arrive at its goals. It is what you do.
The Vision Statement – describes your final destination somewhere in the future. Some would say your *vision* is your *mission* in action.

Suppose we create a fictitious organization to experiment with as we develop our sample Statement of Purpose.

Download at:
ministryTHRIVE.com/IYE/WriteAPurposeStatement.pdf

Blog Post Email Example (pg. 2)

In its simplest form, the Statement of Purpose answers four questions:

1. **Why this need?** What is the problem or need and why does it need to be addressed?
2. **Why this way?** What vital services do we offer to meet the need?
3. **Why us?** Why are we uniquely qualified to solve this hardship?
4. **Why now?** What is the urgency to respond and what will be done with their support?

Now let's answer these four questions for our fictional organization – Project A.N.Y.

Why this need? The orphaned children of the Congo lack the basic needs to help them survive: loving parents, a healthy diet, a safe and secure environment, access to medical care, education, the joy of life itself, and the saving grace that comes from knowing Jesus Christ. Without life's basic essentials these children will parish.

Why this way? Project A.N.Y. plans to construct suitable living conditions. These housing units will be staffed by national caregivers that will love, and look after the children's safety and nourishment. A medical facility will be constructed to care for their health. A school will be established to educate the children. The curriculum will be Christian-based so each child has the opportunity for a solid education and be able to learn about Jesus Christ. Each school will also be equipped with a playground so the children can play and have fun between classes.

Download at:
ministryTHRIVE.com/IYE/WriteAPurposeStatement.pdf

Blog Post Email Example (pg. 3)

Why us? Because of our experience in successfully applying similar solutions to other African villages in the area, we believe Project A.N.Y is well suited to accomplish these goals. In the past 25 years, we have worked closely with African nationals in 10 neighboring villages. These villages are now considered models by the African government and showcased to other non-profits and relief organizations wishing to work in these areas.

Why now? Because of the AIDS epidemic and the strife caused by warring factions in the country, time is of the essence. Today there are 550,000 orphans that go without life's basis needs. This number increases by 8% per year. Without a solution, tens of thousands of children will parish never knowing the joys of life and never hearing about Jesus.

The answers to these four questions are concise and understandable. They could be more complex depending on the goals of the organization and the problems on the ground. Remember, less is more. Add whatever level of complexity is necessary for clarity sake only.

Does your organization's Purpose Statement set you apart?

Copyright © 2018 ministryTHRIVE, All rights reserved.
You are receiving this email because you subscribed to our weekly news brief.

Our mailing address is:
ministryTHRIVE
1559 Portland Gold Dr
Colorado Springs, CO 80905-4407

Add us to your address book

Want to change how you receive these emails?
You can update your preferences or unsubscribe from this list.

Download at:
ministryTHRIVE.com/IYE/WriteAPurposeStatement.pdf

Chapter 29...

Before I Go
(2 MIN READ)

Congratulations! You've made it. ***Ignite Your Email Campaign*** is now on your tool belt. We hope the examples, illustrations, worksheets, and advice shared here helps in: *boosting awareness for your cause, increases your ability to acquire new donors, builds lasting relationships*, and *raises more funds.*

ministryTHRIVE is here if you need further assistance or have a question:

Our in-box is always open:

john@ministryTHRIVE.com

Two more topics before we close ***Ignite Your Email Campaign.***

Emails Cannot Replace Relationships

Can I get personal for a moment? Email is a magnificent communication tool. One person can talk to another person or group at any time anywhere in the world. It can also play the role of a great avoidance tool. No meetings have to be attended. No smartphones have to be dialed. No video chats need activation. People can communicate without actually meeting each other face-to-face.

For instance, fundraising is already challenging enough. But, if a person uses email as a way of avoiding the uncomfortable feelings that go along with calling to set up appointments and making appeals face-to-face, that person may have little success.

It's understood that there is a good chance the non-profit's contacts may be located across a country or around the world. However, technology is eliminating that geographic gap daily.

Video chat programs such as SKYPE and Zoom offset the need to meet face-to-face. Plus, phone calls are still more effective than email.

Yes, use email to establish new contacts. Yes, email can be key to strengthening existing relationships.

Just, don't use email as a way of precluding a more personal touch with donors and potential supporters.

Respond...Respond...Respond

Nothing kills a campaign no matter what the goal: whether boosting awareness, acquiring new names, building stronger relationships, or attempting to raise funds, if the organization is either slow to respond (we're talking glacial speed here) or opts not to reply at all.

Comments on social media need to be answered almost immediately. Comments to blog posts or emails that are sent to an organization need a relatively prompt response as well.

About the Author

John founded ministryTHRIVE in 2018. It's mission: "**Provide exceptional learning experiences to those in ministry to ensure they master the skills necessary to achieve their goals.**"

ministryTHRIVE's plan is to develop and deliver learning materials in eight critical non-profit success areas: administration, management, branding, marketing, communication, engagement, fundraising, and donor relations. Initially, the educational materials will take the form of: articles, eBooks, paperbacks, podcasts, and webinars.

Before ministryTHRIVE, John founded InPlainSite Marketing, a leader in developing and delivering digital marketing strategies. John consulted and presented to Fortune 100 and 500 companies. He is a bestselling author of eighteen books. ***Ignite Your Email Campaign*** is available on Amazon.com and where ever books are sold. His books have been featured in Amazon's Top 10 is the US, Canada, the UK, and Australia. John's musings are regularly picked up by CustomerThink.com, Business2Community.com, TheStreet.com, Entrepreneur.com, Visa Business, *Yahoo!* Finance, MSNBC.com, The Globe and Mail, Reuters, and The New York Daily News.

John has served on the boards of non-profits for more than a dozen years. He has enjoyed leading as either president, chairman of the board, or as a director doing what he can to help organizations succeed. He has also valued his time as a volunteer in the trenches.

As president and chairman of the board, John has helped launch a crisis pregnancy center and thrift shop while living in Illinois. In Colorado, he was asked to be president and chairman of the board for a startup Christian school in Woodland Park. He has also served as a director on the board of an entrepreneurial organization, Middle Market Entrepreneurs, in Colorado Springs. He has served on a leadership council, as creative director and as a church volunteer in many other capacities. John believes his most rewarding times as a volunteer are when he gets to work alongside Kay or one of their children or grandchildren. Today, John's life centers on God, family, church, and community.

John loves spending time with Kay, his bride and best friend of 48 years of marriage. They have three of the greatest kids, okay grownups, on this planet as well as eight grandchildren. John and Kay live in Colorado.

BY
JOHN D. LEAVY

FROM THE IGNITION SERIES:

Ignite Your Fundraising

Available at Amazon.com
or wherever books are sold.

....

Find more great resources at ministryTHRIVE.com.

BY
JOHN D. LEAVY

FROM THE IGNITION SERIES:

**Ignite Your
Donor Passion**

Available at Amazon.com
or wherever books are sold.

....

Find more great resources at ministryTHRIVE.com.

www.ingramcontent.com/pod-product-compliance
Lightning Source LLC
Chambersburg PA
CBHW071528220526
45469CB00003B/689